UNSHAKEABLE

The Perfect Book for Female Leaders

HOW TO BE YOUR MOST
AUTHENTIC &
COURAGEOUS SELF

MIDJA FISHER

To Mum and Dad, who believed in me first.

About Midja

Midja Fisher is an expert in building confidence. She inspires leaders to be authentic, vulnerable and courageous. She is a dynamic speaker and facilitator who shares her personal and professional stories openly and passionately.

Midja is obsessed with partnering with female professionals to discover their purpose, realise their talents and inspire them to step up and take the lead. As a trusted mentor, Midja helps women develop their own authentic leadership style and gain the self-belief they need to take their seat at the leadership table.

Midja's background includes 20 years' experience in the corporate world as a partner of a national law firm and a learning and development specialist.

What's unique about Midja is her infectious energy, enthusiasm and optimism, which are evident in her work and personal life.

ABOUT MIDJA

With her blend of empathy and conviction, Midja challenges her clients to step out of their comfort zones to see what is possible.

Her practice is based on personalised service and a deep understanding of the challenges leaders face. Midja partners with individuals and businesses to create leaders people want to follow, teams people want to play with and organisations people want to belong to.

Midja lives on the Gold Coast with her three kids, Tom, Sophie and Jack, and their cavoodle, DJ. She is a self-confessed sun worshipper, champagne drinker, tap and hip-hop dancer, and lover of life!

You can get in touch with Midja at www.midja.com.au.

Acknowledgements

Confidence starts from within. It's based on how deeply we know ourselves and our degree of self-belief. I was lucky enough to be blessed with two amazing, generous and loving parents, who were the first people to believe in me. To Mum and Dad, thank you for giving me the gift of unconditional love and acceptance. You made me believe I could take on the world. This feeling has always stayed with me. I miss you both every day.

To my own kids, Tom, Sophie and Jack, you're my everything and you're always front of mind in every decision I make. Thank you for your fun, your energy, your honesty and your encouragement. Thank you for putting up with the flipchart in the lounge room, the Post-It notes on the windows and the huge amount of talking I do aloud to myself as I unpack an idea. I know I can sound a little crazy! The thing I'm most grateful for from you guys is that you have shown me so much more about myself. Yes, we test each other at times, there's annoyance and there's frustration, but

ACKNOWLEDGEMENTS

there's an abundance of understanding and love. Keep being your amazing selves. I love sharing my life with you. Thank you.

To my beautiful sister, Rell, I'm so grateful for your support and encouragement and I love the relationship you have with Tom, Sophie and Jack. You've been there for me when I needed you the most and your words of encouragement have lifted my spirits. I don't know what I would do without you.

To Debbie, who can finish my sentences and who seems to know my thoughts before I've even thought of them. I'm so thankful that our lives intertwined and we've become lifelong friends. I love that I can share anything and everything with you. I trust you and respect you and feel so blessed to have you in my life.

To everyone who helped and supported me in writing this book. To my wonderful mentor, Jane Anderson. You have shown me what it takes to live my dream, to follow my passion, and to lead my practice with purpose. To the editing and publishing team, Lauren Shay at Full Stop Writing, Editing and Design and Sylvie Blair at BookPOD, thank you for your commitment and dedication to getting this book out there to my readers.

And to my tribe of women, my amazing girlfriends who are there for me, you know who you are. From the bottom of my heart, I want to say thank you. It's been a ride, hasn't it? The ups and downs, swings and roundabouts. For me, having such a loyal, beautiful, funny, inspirational bunch of women surrounding me has made all the difference. Thank you for sharing your life with me. There have been tears but there have been many more laughs. There's been plenty of "deep and meaningfuls" over a glass or two of wine – talking men, kids, family, career and life. There have been quiet dinners in and wild nights out. You're there for me and you inspire me and I love you.

Finally, to my readers. Thank you for picking up this book and committing to gaining the confidence you need to be the amazing women I know you are.

Midja x

CONTENTS

INTRODUCTION

Introduction

What a year 1997 was for me. It was the start of two of the most important relationships in my life: one was with the man who would become my husband, and the other with the law firm that would become my second family.

I'd just finished university and felt relieved to have finally completed my double degree. Five years of full-time study had felt like an eternity. It was time to put my studies behind me and get out there to make my mark on the world.

I'd secured a place with Pricewaterhouse Urwick (as it was called at the time) in its graduate program. I packed my bags in January and headed to Tampa, Florida, for my 12-week induction course. It was my first time overseas and my first job; a time of trepidation but also great excitement.

It was late at night when I finally arrived at Tampa Airport. I was

INTRODUCTION

walking around aimlessly, looking for the baggage carousel, feeling exhausted and looking like death (flights from Brisbane to Sydney to Auckland to Los Angeles to Dallas to Tampa will do that to you!). I wasn't too tired, however, to spot a tall, handsome man with broad shoulders and a tan, carrying a suitcase in one hand and golf clubs in the other. I smiled at him and he smiled at me. Little did I know that this man was also in Tampa to work for Pricewaterhouse and that in two years' time I would be walking down the aisle to marry him.

We spent 12 weeks together in the US. It was a whirlwind love affair and we returned to Australia knowing we wanted to build a life together. I spent some time working in the Brisbane office, then transferred to Sydney where my soon-to-be husband worked.

It was about six months later when I realised that Pricewaterhouse was not the organisation for me. Once I make my mind up about something, I act quickly. So, I resigned, packed my bags, headed back to Queensland and moved back in with my parents with my partner soon following me.

Ever the optimist, I had no job to go to but knew the right one would come along. And luckily for me, it did. I started my articled clerkship at a law firm and was admitted as a solicitor two years later. A few years after that, I made partner and was living the dream. Work wasn't work for me. I loved it!

I was happily married, living on the Gold Coast, doing work I loved, raising three gorgeous kids and having fun with an amazing group of girlfriends. It was a sweet life. I had a good run.

Fast forward to 2016 and it all came crashing down.

In 2016, I knew that my marriage was over. My husband moved out of our family home – the home we'd built together, on the land we'd bought on our honeymoon. I remember being in the house by myself with the kids and just how different it felt.

In 2016, my time with my second family, the law firm, was also over. At 42 years of age, I was an unemployed single mum with three children. This was not in my mission statement and certainly not on my vision board!

I felt lost, lonely, and above all, rejected. Personally and professionally, I wasn't wanted. It was a real stab to the heart. I was at my lowest. To be frank, I felt like crap. My confidence and self-belief were at rock bottom. If these people didn't want me, who would?

I knew I had to pick myself up. I had no time for a pity party, so what was I going to do? What was missing? Why did I feel like this? I started thinking deeply about myself and my story. I thought back to the old me and I remembered one Christmas family vacation.

I was 12 years old and my family was taking our annual summer holiday on the Gold Coast. It was at a place called Mermaid Lodge at Mermaid Beach. I woke up on Christmas Eve with the idea to put on a Christmas concert down by the pool for everyone in the apartment block, a one-woman show. That was the kind of kid I was. I told Mum and Dad and they were super supportive as always. I drew up the flyers, knocked on all the doors and invited everyone to the concert. I swam in the pool during the day and I talked the concert up to everyone there.

The concert was a huge success – in my eyes, anyway. People sat by the pool, others sat on their balconies and watched. I sang, danced, played my electric keyboard and recited Christmas poetry.

INTRODUCTION

I often think back and wonder, what was going on in that girl's head? She was carefree. She didn't care what people thought of her. It was about having fun. It was about being of service to others and doing something that would bring joy and happiness to other people. There was no self-judgement. There was no self-doubt. She had an idea and she tried it. No fear of failing; she gave everything a go.

In 2016, I had to find that fearless Midja again. The thing that was missing from my life was **confidence**. I felt like it had been knocked out of me. Little did I know my confidence was still inside me and no one could take it away. I just had to work on finding myself again and rebuilding my self-belief. I know I'm not the first woman who has doubted herself, who has felt invisible and lost, and I'm sure I won't be the last.

I'm friends with, have worked with and have admired so many amazing women who have no idea how amazing they are. They just don't see it. The blinkers are well and truly in place. You might be one of these women yourself. You're a woman who has amazing strengths, purpose and magic. You have a gift to give the world to make a difference. You are a woman who has so many opportunities and choices but you may not see them. I wrote this book for you. I've been there, I've felt that, and I've written the book quite literally.

I love to surround myself with women. I love their company and their energy. Don't get me wrong, I like men, too – I have sons who I adore, men who I date, male leaders and colleagues I have loved working with. But there is something about being in a room full of women, sharing stories over a cuppa or, if we get the chance, a glass of wine. There is magic in sharing our common experiences, our problems, our fears and our dreams.

In this book, I share my personal stories in the hope that you will connect with them. There are stories about being a leader, a mother, a daughter, a sister, a lover, a friend.

I believe that as a leader, you don't turn up to work and switch off the other parts of your life. When I walked into the corporate office, Midja the mum, the wife, the daughter, the sister and the friend would all come with me. All our relationships impact the way we feel about ourselves and how we see ourselves. We are a combination of all our experiences, the personal and the professional.

My wish is that this book gives you the inspiration and tools to become your most authentic, courageous, unshakeable self. It contains a lot of common-sense principles, but I know that sometimes, we all need a gentle reminder about how we can live and lead more authentically, more honestly and with purpose and passion. Sometimes things get in the way of our true selves. Often, it's our own thoughts and beliefs.

I hope this book will be dog-eared, highlighted and written in, but most of all I hope it inspires you to believe in yourself and follow your passion. It's time to push your self-doubt and fear to one side and step up to lead with tenacity.

I would love you to share this book with your girlfriends, your mum, your sister, your daughter, your colleagues, that woman in your life who you know is so, so amazing, remarkable and stunning but she doesn't know it. It's our time.

Happy reading.

Midja x

CHAPTER 1

WHY DOES CONFIDENCE MATTER?

CHAPTER 1

Why does confidence matter?

As women, we bring a unique set of skills, behaviours and viewpoints to the leadership table. However, we also harbour a unique set of problems and fears that prevent us from reaching our full potential. In fact, half of all women report feeling self-doubt about their job performance and careers.[1]

WHY AREN'T THERE MORE FEMALE LEADERS?

In Australia, senior management roles and CEO positions continue to be male dominated, with only 16% of CEOs being women and 30% of key management positions held by women.[2] At the current rate of change, recent estimates propose it will take until 2095 to

1 *Ambition and gender at work.* Institute of Leadership and Management, London, 2011. https://30percentclub.org/wp-content/uploads/2014/08/ILM_Ambition_and_Gender_report_0211-pdf.pdf

2 *Australia's gender equality scorecard – Key findings from the Workplace Gender Equality Agency's 2016-17 reporting data.* Workplace Gender Equality Agency, November 2017.

reach gender equality in the workplace.[3] This is despite research that clearly shows gender diversity gives better financial results. Companies with at least 30% female leaders have net profit margins up to 6 percentage points higher than companies with no women in the top ranks.[4] Furthermore, companies in the top quartile for gender diversity are 15% more likely to have financial returns above their national industry medians.[5]

It's clear that having gender diversity at the leadership table is great for business and, as such, it is now a high priority for many organisations. The CEOs I speak to want *more* women on their leadership teams. So why do we still have a gender disparity at senior leadership levels? I believe there is a range of factors at play.

Firstly, there are simply more men in current leadership positions. The human tendency to gravitate towards people like ourselves means that leading men are more likely to sponsor and advocate for other men when leadership opportunities arise. They may not do this deliberately but there is an unconscious bias at play.

Secondly, the lack of female leaders means there are not enough female role models or mentors. Aspiring female leaders need role models they can connect with, whose style and behaviours they can relate to and experiment with. There are simply not enough females in leadership roles to influence emerging female talent.

Thirdly, leadership is typically associated with the traditional

3 Brooke-Marciniak, Schreiber & Twaronite. "Women. Fast Forward. The time for gender parity is now." EY, 2015.

4 Noland, M., Moran, T., Kotschwar, B. *Is Gender Diversity Profitable? Evidence from a Global Survey.* Peterson Institute for International Economics and EY, Washington, 2016. https://piie.com/publications/wp/wp16-3.pdf

5 Hunt, V. "Why diversity matters." McKinsey & Company, January 2015. https://www.mckinsey.com/business-functions/organization/our-insights/why-diversity-matters

masculine traits of assertiveness, independence, competitiveness and decisiveness. Traits considered more feminine, such as empathy, collaboration, intuition and emotion, are not valued as highly when it comes to leadership. In fact, they're often considered counter-productive.

This outdated view of leadership leaves women feeling there is no place for them at the leadership table. They are faced with the following dilemma. On the one hand, they can change their behaviour and become more masculine to fit the leadership mould. If they choose this option, they are often considered an effective leader but are not well liked (cue the "bitch" reference). On the other hand, they can continue to apply their conventional feminine style and be liked as a leader but not seen as an effective one. In this case, they are typically referred to as "soft" or too emotional.

Our perception of leadership needs to change. Women need to stop feeling as though they must take on masculine behaviours to be a successful leader. Masculinity shown by a man is considered real but masculinity shown by a woman is seen as fake. The feedback I've received from women working in corporate positions is that they would much rather have a man as their leader than a woman. When I ask why, their responses are similar: "With a female leader, I feel like I don't know where I stand. They seem insincere, I don't trust them." I have even heard of female leaders described as "smiling assassins". Yikes!

During my own career, I was often told to stop leading from the heart, stop showing too much empathy, toughen up and be decisive. I have talked with many other female leaders who have received similar feedback from their male managers. These types of messages tell women they are not leadership material. In other words, they need to change or step aside. These factors all play a part in the lack of female leadership representation in Australia. A fundamental societal and organisational change needs to happen.

However, I believe there is another compelling reason why not enough women are in leadership roles. And that is the way we see ourselves. Our self-doubt has a lot to answer for.

The great news is that every woman has the power to change this. If we change the way we feel about ourselves, we can influence the way others see women leaders. We must be the change.

Be the change you wish to see in the world.

MAHATMA GANDHI

THE WAY WE SEE OURSELVES

Women often share with me their frustration over the relentless pursuit of balance. You know, that magical space where you have achieved perfect equilibrium in all aspects of your life. Sounds wonderful, right?

Women want to be everything to everyone, but they also feel they're not doing a very good job at *anything*! It's like they have thrown all the balls in the air in an attempt to juggle them but are dropping them one by one. When a woman shares her to-do list with me, I feel exhausted. No wonder they do, too!

As women, we want to be there for others, we care, but we can lose ourselves when we put everyone before us. We put ourselves last on the to-do list. This results in us feeling that we have no energy, no purpose, and that time is running away.

We try to emulate this idea of what it means to be the "perfect" woman. The problem is, this perfect woman doesn't exist.

With all of this going on in our heads, we become fearful. We doubt ourselves and end up feeling like an imposter.

THE IMPOSTER SYNDROME

Over my career, I've had many conversations with friends where we have confessed to feeling like an imposter. These are all highly successful, intelligent, capable women who have felt that they didn't deserve the success they had achieved in their careers.

The term "imposter syndrome" describes the persistent fear of being exposed as a fraud. Sound familiar? It does to me and I'm not alone. Researchers believe that up to 70% of people have suffered from imposter syndrome at some point.[6] It's a common experience.

Imposter syndrome is that voice in your head that says, "What are you doing here? They are going to find you out!"

It may take the form of perfectionism, the belief that you need to be perfect at everything to be successful in your role. You discount praise from others and believe your goals have been achieved

---

6 Warrell, M. "Afraid Of Being 'Found Out'? How To Overcome Imposter Syndrome." *Forbes*, 3 April, 2014. https://www.forbes.com/sites/margiewarrell/2014/04/03/impostor-syndrome/#10d928a748a9

through sheer luck rather than your own efforts. You worry about not being "enough", that people will find out you're a fraud. The fear of failure – the fear you will be unable to deliver and disappoint everyone – can be overwhelming.

These feelings lead to low self-confidence and self-doubt. You dwell on your mistakes and failures. Imposter syndrome keeps you in your comfort zone, under the radar. You don't want to be seen in case you are judged negatively by others. You stay safe and may even sabotage yourself because you don't feel you deserve success.

Despite this, I believe this worry and stress comes from a good place. It means you want to achieve great things. There are many examples of talented people who have suffered from imposter syndrome. Even Academy Award-winning actress Kate Winslet revealed: "I'd wake up in the morning before going out to a shoot and think, I can't do this; I'm a fraud."

Imposter syndrome can arise from aiming high and wanting to do your best. The key is to embrace those feelings and use them to move forward. Take, for example, Nobel laureate and author Maya Angelou, who said: "I have written 11 books, but each time I think, 'Uh oh, they are going to find out now. I've run a game on everybody, and they're going to find me out.'" Even someone as high-achieving as Angelou has had these negative thoughts, but she was able to overcome them, move forward and write a wealth of critically acclaimed books, essays, plays and film and TV scripts.

MY STORY

When I started my legal career in my early 20s, I suffered from imposter syndrome – so much so that I made myself physically sick. I was sure someone was going to approach me and ask me what I was doing there.

The voice in my head said: What do you think you're doing in this office? You, a lawyer? Yeah, sure. You're not a lawyer, you're an imposter. And guess what! At some point, these smart people around you are going to find out. You're going to get a tap on your shoulder, so be ready for it.

In those early days as a law clerk, I would often have to run from my desk into the bathroom to be sick. I was overwhelmed and anxious. I remember sitting on the toilet and breathing, taking some time out for myself, then walking back into the office and getting to work on my files. Sounds crazy, right?

Eight years later, I was made a partner of the firm. During my career, I would often think back to that young Midja, so anxious, scared and unsure of herself, and smile. She wanted to be her best, she wanted to make a difference and she wanted it so badly.

CHAPTER 1

Many of us will feel like an imposter at some time in our life. So, what can we do about it?

We need to ensure these feelings don't cripple us. We can't let them stop us from taking risks; rather, we must recognise them as signals of personal growth and opportunity. It's time to step up and be confident.

THE NIGGLE

In addition to the imposter syndrome, there is another feeling you could be experiencing. It's often buried deep down — the feeling that you want more in life, that you could contribute more, a desire, a dream. I call it the "niggle".

It's the question: what else is possible? The "what if", the "someday I'll ..." It may be so deep inside you that you can't even feel it yet. You might be so caught up in the hectic pace of life that you may not pay it any attention. Conversely, it may be screaming at you, demanding your attention.

I felt the niggle for years. It wouldn't go away. I was reasonably happy with my life. In fact, anyone looking at me would have told me to count my blessings and not upset the apple cart. It felt almost ungrateful to want more, but I did want more. Not more material things; I had everything I needed. I wanted deeper relationships and I wanted to be of greater service to others. I wanted to feel like I was making the difference I was meant to make.

The niggle isn't something you talk about. You don't share these thoughts with others, except maybe those closest to you. Fear of judgement and self-doubt keep these dreams contained.

It's time to let them out.

It's time to build the confidence you need to stop feeling like an imposter. It's time to start listening to the niggle and pursue your purpose.

> *Our deepest fear is not that we are inadequate. Our deepest fear is that we are powerful beyond measure. It is our light, not our darkness, that most frightens us. We ask ourselves, Who am I to be brilliant, gorgeous, talented and fabulous? Actually, who are you not to be?*

MARIANNE WILLIAMSON

THE POWER OF CONFIDENCE

It has been identified that there is a "crisis of confidence" experienced by women as they build their career.[7] Both men and women start their careers equally confident of reaching senior management but after just two years, this confidence remains stable for men but diminishes for women. As women gain experience, their confidence falls by half.[8]

As a result, many talented and amazing women leave the corporate world or become stagnant in their careers, never making the next step up to executive level.

As a female leader, building and maintaining confidence is the key to achieving your goals and making the difference you are meant to make. Confidence builds resilience and allows you to step outside your comfort zone to take risks and challenge yourself. You *can* be creative, agile and open to change. When you no longer focus on self-doubt, you can focus on being of service to others and changing lives.

Confidence improves your thinking and influence as a leader. It greatly increases your career prospects and you are more likely to rise in seniority. It's that secret ingredient to being able to stand up and say, "It's my turn." Confidence gives you clearer focus and direction. You know where you want to go and how to get there.

Without confidence, you are dependent on others. Your self-worth

---

7 Coffman, J. and Neuenfeldt, B. "Everyday Moments of Truth: Frontline Managers are Key to Women's Career Aspirations." Bain & Company, 2014. http://www.bain.com/publica-tions/articles/everyday-moments-of-truth.aspx

8 Coffman, J. and Neuenfeldt, B. "Everyday Moments of Truth: Frontline Managers are Key to Women's Career Aspirations." Bain & Company, 2014. http://www.bain.com/publica-tions/articles/everyday-moments-of-truth.aspx

is tied up in what other people think of you. You settle for less than you deserve, personally and professionally. As a beautiful friend of mine, Simone, reminded me recently, "Midja, we haven't gone through all this to settle." No, we haven't, Simone!

When you lack confidence, you give up. Everything seems too hard and you make excuses for yourself. You justify to yourself and others why some people have been able to achieve fulfilment and success but you haven't. You might also blame others for what you consider the injustices in your life.

You stay "under the radar" in your career. You play it safe, not drawing attention to yourself, hoping to remain unnoticed and continue doing what you've always been doing. This may be a comfortable place to stay for a while, but it won't fulfil you in the long term.

Effective leaders have the perfect balance of confidence and humility. Their self-confidence allows them to show modesty and empathy towards others. They're not threatened by the success of others around them and they reward collaboration.

In my work with women, I find they are often out of balance. They have an abundance of humility but not enough confidence.

THE FIVE LEVELS OF CONFIDENCE

To become a confident female leader, you need to know where you are positioned now. Where do you rate on the Confidence Scale?

CONFIDENCE SCALE

	TYPE	OBSTACLE	FOCUS	CONFIDENCE %
5	Unshakeable	Sustainability	Reconnection	100%
4	Growing	Doubt	Self-belief	50%
3	Steady	Trust	Authenticity	25%
2	Precarious	Clarity	Self-awareness	10%
1	Lost	Negativity	Motivation	-10%

LOST

At this lowest level of confidence, you have a **negative** sense of self and your life circumstances. As a result, you feel **lost** and hopeless, like there is no way out of your current situation. You play the victim, blaming others for your lack of motivation and inability to move forward in your life. You feel out of control and unable to make positive choices. You feel powerless.

You're isolated from others and feel alone. You have little interest in life, both personally and professionally, and feel there is little to look forward to.

Professionally, you're unable to make a positive contribution to the workplace. You're viewed as pessimistic, unhelpful and obstructive.

At this level of confidence, you need **motivation** to re-engage with yourself and the world around you. You require a dramatic shift in thinking and a strong desire to change.

PRECARIOUS

At this level, you lack **clarity** about who you are – your purpose, your values, your strengths and how you can contribute. You don't feel like you know yourself anymore, which means your confidence is at a **precarious** point.

You may find yourself at this level when you have experienced a significant change in your life and are searching for a new identity. This could be due to a relationship breakdown, a significant change at work, a new role in your life (for example, as a mother or carer of an elderly parent), or it might simply be that you've come to a point in your life where you feel there is another layer to yourself. It's like you've been cruising through life, knowing yourself and everything is rosy, then BAM! You realise, "Wait a minute, there's more to know about me."

At this level on the Confidence Scale, you're highly dependent on others. You rely on their opinion of you to feed your self-worth. It's difficult for you to make decisions and you often allow others to make them for you. You're unsure of yourself, unsteady on your feet and can be highly critical of yourself.

As a leader with this level of confidence, you second guess yourself. As a result, you are inconsistent with your decision making. Your people are unsure of what is expected of them and your team lacks direction and purpose.

To move up the scale, your focus needs to be on **self-awareness** – getting to know yourself.

STEADY

You have a deep understanding of who you are. You know your personal values and beliefs, you have a clear purpose and you understand your talents and strengths. You know yourself, but you lack the courage to *show* yourself.

At this level, you're still somewhat dependant on others. You're **steady** in your behaviour. You're cautious and stay in your comfort zone. You might experience some inner conflict because you know who you are, but you don't feel you can fully express yourself. You hold back and agree with others when inside you feel differently.

A lack of **trust** prevents you from expressing the real, authentic you. This might be due to a new relationship, situation or challenge in your personal or professional life. This situation or relationship is unfamiliar to you and trust is still being built. You might call this the "honeymoon" period. When you start a new role or new relationship, you want to please and impress. This means there might be parts of yourself and your personality that you hold back. It's like you're holding your breath. Then, little by little, as the relationship grows and your confidence builds, you're able to let your breath out and be yourself.

At this level of confidence, you need to focus on being yourself.

Express your viewpoint, use your strengths and talents to lead and influence and let your **authenticity** shine.

GROWING

When you are **growing**, you know yourself and can be yourself. However, you're often held back from reaching your full potential. This is because knowing yourself is not the same as knowing how amazing you are.

At this level, even though you are authentic and congruent as a leader, you **doubt** yourself and your abilities. There is that negative voice in your head saying you're not enough.

It's time to leave your comfort zone to see what you're truly capable of. You need to stop the comparisons and step into the spotlight. Become a true leader worth following.

To do this, your focus needs to be on building your **self-belief**.

UNSHAKEABLE

At this highest level of confidence, you're **unshakeable**. You have an unwavering self-belief and can be truly authentic in all situations.

As a leader, you show resilience and courage. You are strong, inspirational and have a presence that makes people feel better about themselves. Your confidence influences those around you.

You deal with stress effectively and see obstacles as challenges rather than excuses. You've done the hard work on yourself and now you can focus on your people and your purpose. You use your confidence to serve others and achieve your goals.

Once you reach this level of confidence, you need to **sustain** it. There will always be challenges and changes in your life that may cause you to question yourself. These circumstances may threaten to knock your confidence back down to precarious. Don't let them. Continually **reconnect** with yourself, your values and your beliefs. Keep being true to yourself, lead authentically and maintain your belief in yourself and your gift to the world.

DIVERSITY IN LEADERSHIP

We need a robust pipeline of confident women to take their seat at the leadership table. We need to work with men to change traditional views of leadership. Real diversity is what's needed. Masculinity and femininity make a powerful combination; united, they bring a range of valuable skills, behaviours and viewpoints to the leadership table.

As women, we need to connect with one another, talk openly about our experiences, share what we've learnt and support each other.

As a leader, it's time to grow your confidence and leadership skills. Seize opportunities to expand and challenge yourself. You will transform your self-perception and you will start to feel and act like a leader. You will lead from an authentic space, knowing there is absolutely no need to change who you are. You are enough – in fact, you are more than enough.

We hold ourselves back in ways both big and small, by lacking self-confidence, by not raising our hands, and by pulling back when we should be leaning in.

SHERYL SANDBERG

CONFIDENCE FOR FEMALE LEADERS

CHAPTER 2

Confidence for female leaders

The toughest part of being a leader is the work you need to do on yourself. To become unshakeable takes time and effort. It takes determination to put in the hard work to discover who you are as a leader and develop your leadership brand. You must prioritise your self-development, but don't mistake self-focus for self-absorption.

A confident leader uses their power to be of service to others, to make the difference they are meant to make. It's not about vanity or egotism. Effective leadership is navigating the balance between self-confidence and humility. It's about believing in yourself and your legacy but also believing in and valuing your people.

For women to gain the confidence they need to inspire and lead, they must fulfil three critical areas of self-development:

1. KNOW YOURSELF

The first step to gaining confidence is to truly know yourself. You need to heighten your *self-awareness* and understand the real you. It's about gaining clarity on your leadership identity.

2. BE YOURSELF

The next step is to be yourself. Show yourself to the world. This is about embracing your authenticity and learning how to fully *self-express*. This is when you develop a strong authentic leadership brand that connects with your purpose.

3. BELIEVE IN YOURSELF

The final step is to believe in yourself. This is when you develop an unwavering *self-belief* in who you are and what you can achieve. It's gaining the leadership mindset to realise your full potential and reach your goals.

The following chapters in this book will explore these three key areas of self-development in great detail. The Confidence Model demonstrates how they overlap and work together to achieve unshakeable confidence.

THE CONFIDENCE MODEL

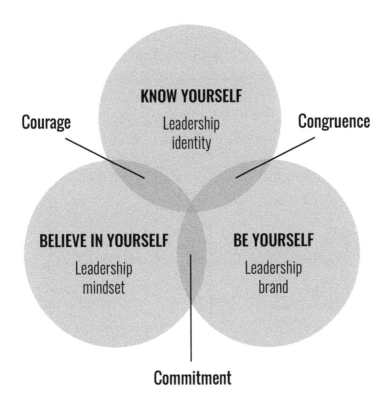

At the intersection of **Know Yourself** and **Be Yourself** is *congruence*. This is where a harmony exists between who you are on the inside and who you are on the outside. Your behaviour and actions match your values and beliefs. There is a real internal and external compatibility. You are transparent and honest as a leader and are genuine about your feelings and experiences.

At the intersection of **Be Yourself** and **Believe in Yourself** is *commitment*. In this space, you have a strong belief in yourself and your purpose, which you share passionately with others. You have a clear intention and focus. You concentrate your time and energy on what is most important to you. You are true to your word and honour your promises, building trust and loyalty as a leader.

Finally, at the intersection of **Believe in Yourself** and **Know Yourself** is *courage*. This is where you know yourself well enough and believe in yourself strongly enough to have a willingness to confront your fears. You'll take a risk, even if it means going against what others think and stepping outside your comfort zone. You're bold, daring and brave. You face your challenges and see them as opportunities. You are a creative and innovative leader who always looks forward.

Courage doesn't always roar.
Sometimes courage is the quiet voice
at the end of the day saying,
"I will try again tomorrow."

MARY ANNE RADMACHER

THE CONFIDENCE TREE

Confidence comes from within. It must develop from your character, from the ground up.

To explain, last Christmas holidays, I took some time out. One of the things I enjoyed doing was taking our cute and sometimes crazy cavoodle, DJ, for a late afternoon walk. Each afternoon as we headed into the park, we passed a house with a tree out the front. This tree had been propped up by several stakes. Every time I walked past, I would think about what it took to be a strong, confident and unshakeable leader – a leader who doesn't need to be propped up as this tree was. I came to realise it takes a strong root system and trunk. In other words, unshakeable leadership requires strong self-awareness, self-expression and self-belief.

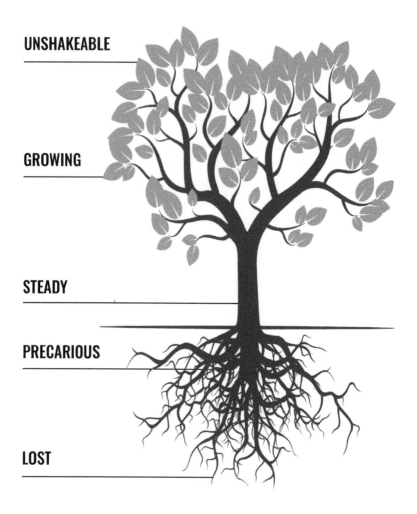

This is the confidence tree. Deep underground is the **lost** level of confidence. This is where the tree is yet to begin to grow. The roots of the tree have yet to sprout. You need motivation and a willingness to begin to develop the tree.

At the base of the tree is the **precarious** level of confidence. This is where the roots of the tree grow. The roots need to be strong enough to support the rest of the tree, otherwise, it can't grow and flourish. This level is about getting to know yourself. The roots are your values, your beliefs, the way you see the world, your legacy and your talents.

The next level of the tree is the trunk – the **steady** level of confidence. The roots of the tree are now secure. You know yourself well and you can start to show yourself to the rest of the world. You're starting to be the real you.

The next level is the base of the branches – the **growing** level of confidence. The trunk of the tree and the roots are now secure, and you are starting to branch out. It's a time of exploration and first growth, where new branches and leaves develop. Now that you know yourself and can be yourself, you're starting to believe in yourself to realise your full potential.

The final level of the tree is the top – the **unshakeable** level of confidence. The tree is now strong. It's been well tended to, looked after and maintained. It is mature. It bears fruits, flowers and an abundance of leaves. It is now time to focus on reconnecting with yourself and your purpose to strengthen your self-belief and maintain your confidence. The tree needs to well-nurtured to remain healthy and strong.

The goal is to get to the top of the tree. Unshakeable confidence takes time and an investment in your personal development. It's important you take this time to ensure a strong foundation. You don't want to grow a tree that is top heavy. If your confidence is based on ego, you are artificially propping up your tree. You have self-belief, but it's not based on who you truly are.

When you don't know who you are and you can't be yourself, you must tie stakes to your trunk, just as my neighbour had to with their tree. You don't have enough root structure or a strong enough trunk to stand tall.

These artificial props can take many forms, such as:

- Your physical appearance: *I'll be confident if I wear the right clothes, make-up and killer heels.*
- Your friends: *I'll be confident if I hang out with the cool gang and do what they do.*
- Your possessions: *I'll be confident if I drive the right car, live in the right suburb and have the latest iPhone.*

Now, I'm not saying there is anything wrong with these things. I love getting dressed up and wearing killer heels. I love nice things (such as my rose-gold MacBook Air!). And I also hang out with the cool gang – my girlfriends are awesome! These are wonderful things to have in your life. But the critical question is, without these props, would you still stand strong? Would you be unshakeable? Or would you sway in the breeze, lean from side to side and eventually fall over?

Where does your confidence come from? Confidence is only real and sustainable if it comes from knowing yourself intimately. You need to be able to show your real self to the world.

When you're at the lower levels of the confidence tree, the top can seem unreachable. It takes time to grow the tree, but you *can* do it. And once you've worked through the lower levels, you will become unshakeable. Your tree will be strong. You will be the confident leader you're meant to be.

CHAPTER 3

KNOW YOURSELF

CHAPTER 3

Know yourself

Genuine and lasting confidence is based on a firm foundation of who you are. The confidence tree starts with strong roots. This means developing a solid sense of self. Getting to know yourself and finding your identity as a leader can be confronting work, yet the rewards are boundless.

To truly know yourself, you need to hold a mirror and take a long, hard look at yourself. Sometimes, just the thought of holding that mirror can be scary! It's like when I've had a big night out with the girls – I wake up, catch a glimpse of myself in the mirror and think, "Argh! Who is that?" My hair has succumbed to the dreaded cowlick, I have panda eyes and it looks like I've aged about 10 years. Yep, sometimes you may not want to look in the mirror, you may not like what you see, but it's necessary if you want to gain a deeper level of self-awareness.

If you don't put in the time and energy to get to know yourself, your confidence tree won't develop deep roots. You'll base your self-worth on what others think of you. Your identity will come from the expectations and views of others, not from who you truly are. Your confidence level will remain lost or precarious and you will be constantly unsure of yourself and your direction.

Without knowing yourself, you second guess your decisions, or worse – you let others make decisions for you. Eventually, you will lose touch with yourself completely. What you need in life to be fulfilled and happy will remain unknown to you.

Gaining full self-awareness requires you to peel back your layers to discover what's underneath.

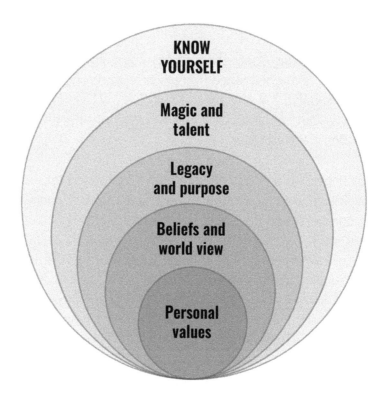

Your inner layer is your **personal values**. These are your preferences and priorities, which provide you with meaning and motivation. Some examples of values include family and belonging, financial success, empathy and intimacy.

These values shape your **beliefs and world view**, which influence your behaviour and decision making. The way each of us sees the world and interprets events is different. We all have a unique point of view and opinion.

Your **legacy and purpose** are your why. Why do you get up every morning? In the words of author and marketing guru Simon Sinek, "Working hard for something you don't care about is called stress. Working hard for something that you love is called passion." Focussing on your legacy allows you to live a fulfilled life.

Your **magic and talent** are what make you unique. These are skills that come naturally to you. They are your strengths.

Understanding these parts of yourself allows you to gain a deep level of self-awareness, discover the real you and build strong roots. In this chapter, you will learn how to:

- Discover your values
- Know your story
- Define your legacy
- Find your magic
- Take time out
- Learn through reflection
- Reduce your choices
- Focus on your priorities
- Try new things
- Reboot your life

The most adventurous journey
to embark on; is the journey to
yourself, the most exciting thing
to discover; is who you really are,
the most treasured pieces that you
can find; are all the pieces of you,
the most special portrait you can
recognise; is the portrait of
your soul.

C. JOYBELL C.

CHAPTER 3.1

Discover your values

Find your meaning and motivation

One of the keys to knowing yourself and having your own sense of identity is knowing your personal values. Your values form your foundation. They are part of the roots of your confidence tree.

Values are your preferences and priorities in life. They provide you with meaning and motivation. All of us have them, whether we're aware of them or not. Your values help you make sense of your world and interpret your life experiences and events. Pretty handy things!

It's important you don't mistake values for morals or ethics. Morals are principles of what is right and wrong. They are judgements, whereas values are neither right nor wrong. They simply are.

CHAPTER 3.1

Ethics are an accepted set of standards or behaviours, usually developed by a professional society within a particular profession. For example, as a solicitor I had an ethical duty to act in the best interests of a client at all times and be honest and courteous in all dealings in the course of legal practice.

Ethics govern and constrain your behaviour. Values also impact your behaviour, but two people can share the same value and be motivated to behave in a different way. For example, think about the value of family and belonging. This is usually a high-priority value for a new mum, and it's also a high-priority value for a member of the Mafia! It's safe to assume the behaviours associated with this value would vary considerably between these two people.

In the words of Paul Chippendale, founder of Minessence International Cooperative: "It doesn't matter what values you have, what matters is how you live them." As you can see from the above example, the same value can be lived in very different ways.

So, where do your values come from? They are formed by many factors, including your age, gender, education, IQ, experiences, upbringing, culture, family, peers, the environment and your work. Your values are personal and will change over time.

Each of us is driven by our values. They guide our decision making and behaviour, whether we like it or not. Your power comes from being able to move your values from your unconscious to your conscious mind. In other words, when you know what your values are, you have greater control over your decisions and direction. You can use your values to increase your self-awareness, know yourself at a deeper level, define your purpose, gain clarity and become fully committed to your work as a leader.

If you've ever had a goal you just couldn't achieve, or if you've ever lacked the motivation to put in the hard yards, chances are the goal wasn't connected to one of your high-priority personal values. It might have been something you thought you "should" do, but because it wasn't linked to your values, there was no real drive to achieve it. It held no significant meaning for you. If you want to succeed with your goal-setting, make sure you link each of your goals to one of your top values.

Your values filter the way you see the world. For example, let's say an opportunity to work interstate is presented to two people. If one of them has a high value of family and belonging, they may feel anxious because it means they'll be away from their partner or children. However, if the other person has a high value of financial security and the work means a wage increase, they might jump at the chance.

Your values also dictate what excites you and what bores you. When I'm in a meeting or at a friend's barbecue, I like to observe people's reactions to the conversation. As soon as someone's eyes light up or I see them get on the defensive, I know the conversation has hit one of their top values – or a nerve! You can't help but react when your values are impacted.

Another advantage of knowing your values is that it's easier to seek companies, businesses, community projects and work opportunities that connect with you. If you can align your personal values and your work, then bingo! You create flow. This is when work doesn't feel like work – you're on point, you're in the zone, you can work for hours on end and you don't know where the time has gone. Have you ever felt this way? If you have, it means your work has connected with your values.

CHAPTER 3.1

Remember, as a leader, your values are the key to influencing and understanding your people. Knowing your own values as a leader means you can be authentic and build trust with others.

Without knowing your values, you struggle to understand your own biases and view of the world. If your values are stuck in your subconscious, it's difficult to understand why you react the way you do. You might ask yourself, "Why do I struggle being motivated doing this type of work? Why am I procrastinating? Why am I reacting so negatively? Why does this new work policy push my buttons?"

If we don't consciously connect with our values, we can't put into words our why, our purpose or how we feel. And when we can't do that, we fail to make our feelings known to others. Values make communication and understanding as a leader so much easier.

So, take the time to discover your personal values. The leading values profiling tool I use is the Minessence Values Framework. This framework consists of a set of 128 values and their descriptors, which are maintained and continually developed by an international group of experts. You can complete an online questionnaire that processes your responses to create your personalised values map, identifying which of the 128 possible values are a priority for you.

You can also gain a more informal view of your values by asking yourself questions associated with your preferences and priorities (see the values exercise).

Your personal values are an integral part of who you are. As a leader, it's essential you gain a clear understanding of your values, share them with others and keep them front of mind in your everyday decision making.

VALUES EXERCISE

To identify your values:

- Think of a time when you felt completely at ease and fulfilled. What was it about the situation that made you feel like this?

_____

_____

_____

_____

- Think of a time when someone or something irritated you and pushed your buttons. What made you feel this way?

_____

_____

_____

_____

- If you had to move to another planet and could only take five things with you, what would they be? Why? What do those five things represent to you?

_____

_____

_____

_____

- Considering your answers to these questions, write down what you consider to be your top five values.

_____

_____

_____

_____

Once you've identified your values, ask yourself:

- Do you have opportunities in your life to experience these values?

_____

_____

_____

- What are these opportunities?

_____

_____

_____

_____

- What extra activities or experiences could you add to your life to experience more of these values?

_____

_____

_____

_____

Until you make the unconscious conscious, it will direct your life and you will call it fate.

CARL JUNG

CHAPTER 3.2

Know your story

What's already been written?

Your story is unique. It's yours and it's full of learning and wisdom. Whether you're aware of it or not, you attribute meaning to all the important events in your life and that meaning shapes you and becomes a part of who you are.

Of course, the same event or circumstance can mean different things to different people. The great thing is that you get to connect the dots the way you want to. You don't have to worry about anyone else's interpretation, just your own. For example, people can work in the same organisation, even in the same team, and take away something different. The same goes for siblings in a family; they have experienced the same upbringing and family events, but they may interpret those events differently and take a different meaning from them.

CHAPTER 3.2

Your story gives you a valuable insight into your why, your beliefs, your values and your behaviours. Your story up until this point has shaped who you are as a leader. The important events of your life have contributed to your leadership style. They have also created your leadership message to the world.

You have gained a range of skills and knowledge from your experiences and the obstacles you've overcome. You've learned from the good times and bad. It's important to take the time to look at the events, encounters and circumstances that have brought you to where you are today. There is value in examining your life story. As a leader, it can help you elevate your thinking and understand what you bring to the leadership table.

While examining your story, look for patterns in your life. Sometimes, we find ourselves learning the same lessons over and over. You may repeat the same behaviours, even though they may not be working for you. You may have the same kind of relationships. Without examining your story, you fail to see the behaviours that worked for you in the past may not be working for you now. Why is that? What's changed? No doubt a lot has changed, but you haven't adjusted your behaviour accordingly.

As you get to know your story, examine the times of transition in your life. When did they occur and why? How did you deal with them? What did the "before and after" look like?

Look for gaps in your life story. Has something been missing, something you have needed? What do you plan to do about it? Start closing the gap between what has happened in your story and where you want the story to end.

Consider the people who have been the greatest influencers at different times of your life. Who has influenced you the most? Why were they a part of your life at that time? What did you learn from them?

Of course, you can't change your past story. The past is the past. But you can gain great insight from it. You don't want to spend too much time dwelling on it or losing yourself in thoughts of what might have been, "if only I had done that ..." Knowing your story is not about navel-gazing or paralysis by analysis; rather, it's about keeping the process light, acknowledging your past events, understanding them, and learning what you can to gain a better understanding of yourself. Use this knowledge to move forward and focus on the future. There may be times when focussing on a past event in great detail can be beneficial and that's part of the counselling process. If this is the case, I recommend you seek counsel from a professional.

If you don't take some time out to know your story, you will struggle to gain that deeper understanding of who you are and how you got here. You'll continue to feel frustrated and confused about why you react the way you do in certain situations. You question yourself, "Where did that response come from?", "Why do I feel like this?" or, "Why does this keep happening to me?"

Your story evolves, it keeps being written and re-written. So, too, are your beliefs, values and behaviours. Your story gives your life context. It doesn't give you an excuse to blame, play the victim or whinge, but it does make you say, "Ah, that's why I think this way and that's why it's one of my values." It allows you to be kinder to yourself, make changes in your life and take deliberate action to form new habits if you want a different direction for your future.

Your past can weigh heavily on you if you don't acknowledge and accept it. It can consume your thoughts and sap your energy. There's a beautiful quote by Susan Gale, who says, "Sometimes you just have to make peace with your past in order to keep your future from becoming a constant battle." It's about not letting the past define you but understanding it so you can make informed choices. It's another self-awareness tool to keep in your toolkit.

So, think about your story. What has shaped you? How has your story influenced you as a person and as a leader? Your story will give you a greater appreciation and understanding of yourself so you can lead with confidence.

HOW DO YOU EXAMINE YOUR STORY?

Consider the events in your life that have triggered strong emotions, either positive or negative. When have you felt happiness, joy, pride, guilt, loss, fear, resentment? The events that have given rise to these emotions are the ones that have mattered the most. They've created the memories you hold near and dear. They're the events that have shaped you.

_____

_____

_____

_____

_____

_____

Consider your childhood loves, your interests, your family (parents, grandparents, siblings), schooling, geography, where you grew up, where you travelled to, your role models, your influences and your work history.

_____

_____

_____

_____

_____

_____

For each story, event or experience, ask yourself:

1. What was the circumstance?

_____

_____

_____

_____

_____

2. What did it mean to me at the time?

_____

_____

_____

_____

_____

3. What is the learning or result?

_____

_____

_____

_____

ONE OF MY STORIES

I grew up in Ipswich on Braeside Hill. I had a very close family, and by close, I mean we lived side by side! To the right was Pop and Nan's home. To the left was Uncle Keith and Auntie Bebe and their four kids. Behind us was my Great Auntie Ivy's house, then there was us: Mum, Dad and four kids. There were no fences between our houses and as kids we were free to roam. In the mornings, I would visit Auntie Bebe at her house and she would braid or plait my hair for school. I remember spending afternoons in Aunt Ivy's back room, having dress fittings and looking at fabrics. She was a gifted seamstress. During my childhood, there was always someone to play with and someone to talk to.

What did this mean to me at the time?

It meant safety, security and love. I always felt that I was surrounded by my tribe – and, quite literally, I was.

What was my learning or the result of this?

The positive impact of this story is that I value family. I strive to create a strong bond with my children. I want to give them the same feelings of safety and security I had as a child. My story has certainly impacted my decision to have three children, and maybe, if given the chance, I would have added a couple more to the brood.

I also know it has impacted how I feel about being alone. I'm still not comfortable with it, but I'm getting better.

CHAPTER 3.2

Sometimes when I'm alone and feeling lonely, I'll say to myself, "Midja, you're not up on the hill anymore." And I laugh because I get it. I understand why I feel the way I do. It's because of my story. It's because of my past experience.

Knowing that my childhood has shaped who I am helps me keep these feelings light. I can decide what I need to do about them, or if I need to do anything about them. It's in my power to change my reactions and feelings.

Loving ourselves through the process of owning our story is the bravest thing we'll ever do.

BRENÉ BROWN

CHAPTER 3.3

Define your legacy

What's your impact on the world?

Sadly, in 2017, I attended the funerals of several people close to me – including my Dad's. As I stood in the church, looking around at my family and friends, listening to the stories shared during the service and later over a few beers, my heart burst with love and pride. My dad's life was a life well spent, and he left an everlasting impact on others.

Later that night, when I was alone and tucked up in bed, my thoughts turned to my own funeral. I asked myself, "Would the people present have warm hearts and fond memories? What would they say about me and my legacy? How would I be remembered?"

When you define your legacy, you give your life purpose. You can live with a clear objective. You know who you are and what your life is about. Your legacy gives you clarity on your decision making. It helps you decide when to say yes and when to say no – something that can be tough to do in our busy lives. Your legacy makes your life choices so much easier. All you need to do is ask yourself, "Does this contribute to who I am and how I want to make a difference?"

None of us live forever, but what does live on is the impact we have on other people's lives and the difference we make. Our legacy is the end-game. You can't take anything with you when you die; all that matters is what you leave behind.

I think all of us could tell a story about someone we will never forget, someone who changed our lives for the better, and who has, therefore, touched the lives of so many others.

For some people, the impact they make will be public and far-reaching – perhaps on the world stage. For others, like my Dad, their impact will be the profound difference they make in the lives of those closest to them: their inner circle, their partner, their friends, their children and their colleagues.

The nature of your impact doesn't matter. It is personal and unique to you. What is important is that your legacy connects with your values, your priorities and what you believe in.

Defining your legacy is like beginning with the end in mind, which is Habit 2 in Dr Stephen Covey's book, *The 7 Habits of Highly Effective People*. If you can define your purpose and the difference you want to make, you can start making your legacy a reality now by putting into place congruent thoughts, behaviours and actions.

If your legacy is not defined, you risk spending your time and energy on things that don't truly matter. You can end up living a life of regret and what-ifs.

Often, people don't consider their legacy until they face a life-changing event or even their own mortality. When this happens, some people look back on their lives with satisfaction, content knowing they wouldn't change a thing. Others feel compelled to make changes immediately, if they still have the opportunity. They want to ensure they say and do the things that matter, the things that will leave a lasting impact.

I was at a breakfast one morning at Palm Beach on the Gold Coast. A beautiful older woman sat across from me. We all had to introduce ourselves: our name, what we did and why we were there. There were some truly inspiring women with amazing stories and dreams for their future. After the introductions, this woman turned to me and said, "Listening to that, I wish I could have my time again." As she said those words, her smile faded and she looked sad, her eyes full of regret. I said to her that it was not too late to write a different story.

You can't change your past, but you still have time to make the difference you want to make. You can create the legacy you want. It's about taking the time to define and discover what that legacy is, then committing yourself to the necessary steps to ensure it comes true. There is no time for regret.

Defining your legacy and finding your purpose means you will live a life of fulfilment. This doesn't necessarily mean your life will always be full of rainbows, unicorns and happy thoughts. It seems to me we can be too preoccupied trying to pursue a life of pure happiness. Of course, happiness is wonderful, but is the pursuit of endless happiness achievable? Shouldn't we instead focus our time and energy on purpose and fulfilment? If we live our legacy, happiness will naturally follow.

In his book, *Man's Search for Meaning*, Viktor Frankl, the great Jewish-Austrian psychiatrist, said: "Man's main concern is not to gain pleasure or to avoid pain but rather to see a meaning in his life." At specific times in our lives, we may not experience happiness, but we will still have a purpose, and that gives us fulfilment. When I looked after my Dad when he was unwell and near the end of his life, was it a happy time? Was I filled with joy? Was it pleasurable? No. But it was a time of great meaning and purpose for me. It was part of my legacy, and that was more than enough. That purpose got me up in the morning. When we don't know our legacy, when we don't know why we're here, we are without purpose. Sure, short bursts of happiness and pleasure are terrific. But in the end, it will be our meaning and legacy that matter most to us.

So, how can you gain clarity on your legacy? Start with the following questions.

QUESTIONS TO DEFINE YOUR LEGACY

1. Name three to five of the most significant people in your life and ask yourself, "What would I like them to say about me? How would I want to be described?"

    _____

    _____

    _____

    _____

    _____

2. Imagine a banner with your name on it and three words underneath. What would those three words be?

    _____

    _____

    _____

    _____

3. If a movie was made about your life, what would be the title and why?

    _____

    _____

    _____

    _____

    _____

4. "One day your life will flash before your eyes. Make sure it's worth watching." – Gerard Way. What would feature on your life's highlight reel?

_____

_____

_____

_____

_____

_____

_____

Doesn't everything die at last, and too soon? Tell me, what is it you plan to do with your one wild and precious life?

MARY OLIVER, THE SUMMER DAY

CHAPTER 3.4

Find your magic

It's inside each of us

Your magic is unique to you. If you can find it and use it to its fullest potential, you can make the difference you are meant to make in the world.

Your magic will contribute to your greatest strength as a leader. It will be what you're known for. Your magic will captivate others and it will build your reputation and brand, allowing you to leave your legacy. It's the gift you have to share with the world.

It reminds me of the story of the Disney fairies. As you might know (particularly if you have young daughters), there are different types of fairies in Pixie Hollow. There are water fairies, animal fairies, light fairies and tinkers – fairies who like to make and fix things. The most famous fairy of all, of course, is Tinker Bell – with her blonde hair, blue eyes, emerald green dress and rebellious nature. Tinker Bell's problem was that she didn't want to be a tinker fairy. Oh, no! She fought against it all the way. She desperately wanted to be a different type of fairy. She looked at the other fairies, saw what they did and wanted to be like them. She envied them. She didn't realise she had her own unique gift.

She tried her hand at other fairy skills but no matter how much she wanted to succeed, she failed. You see, Tinker Bell had a talent, a skill, a magic inside her she couldn't fight. She was a tinker. Tinkering was her gift to the world.

Now, Tinker Bell was determined and tenacious. Once she accepted that she was a tinker, she decided to bring her own unique style to the tinker role.

It's the same with your magic (or your talent, natural skill, strength, whatever you want to call it). You can make it your own. If you fight against your magic, it feels unnatural. Life becomes hard. You feel that you're wasting your time and not moving forward but you're also not sure what you're supposed to be doing. It gnaws at you. You know there is something more you must give, but you don't know what it is. It's your job to find that magic.

I've mentored leaders who, like Tinker Bell, have tried to fight their natural skill, their magic. One female leader had a real gift for attention to detail. She was a perfectionist by nature. She could pick up an error, conduct a SWOT analysis and assess a situation for gaps like no one else, but she hated her talent and thought it was boring. She believed anyone could do what she did. But they couldn't. For her, it was innate. Whether you want to argue for nature or nurture or a combination, it doesn't matter. She had a gift. So, my advice to her was to embrace her gift and make it her own. She needed to bring her personality and her brand to it, just like Tinker Bell. Knowing yourself means finding and accepting your talent and gift.

Sometimes, your magic will find you. It's easy to recognise and identify. But sometimes, it's hidden deep inside and only the right circumstances or opportunity will bring it out. Finding your magic may mean trying new things and seeing what feels right.

So, what type of fairy you are you? What's your magic and how can you use it to become a leader worth following?

HOW TO FIND YOUR MAGIC

1. What do people in your organisation and team come to you for? Is it for your positivity, empathy, decisiveness, humour, attention to detail, determination, bravery or reasoning? Perhaps it's a skill, such as writing, speaking or selling. Whatever it is, pay attention to it.

    _____

    _____

    _____

    _____

    _____

2. What comes naturally to you? I like to call this the "duh" moment. It's that thing you do, say or feel that you think is easy. It's something you think everyone does. But guess what? It's not what everyone does. It's what you do. It's so natural to you that you don't even have to think about it. You don't realise it's your magic. You may not place any value on it because it doesn't take much effort. It's time to take notice of this talent and not ignore it.

    _____

    _____

    _____

    _____

    _____

3. What do you love doing? What's the best part of your day? What's that thing you do at work that doesn't feel like work? I hear people say they would continue to do a certain type of work or an aspect of their job even if they didn't get paid for it. What is this for you?

_____

_____

_____

_____

_____

_____

4. What excites you? What gets your adrenaline going? What do you look forward to? There might be some anxiety and fear around it, but it's that mixture of excitement and fear you need to recognise and identify.

_____

_____

_____

_____

_____

_____

It is important to remember that we all have magic inside us.

J.K. ROWLING

CHAPTER 3.5

Take time out

Solitude

Solitude is the soul's holiday.

I read this quote a while ago and it has stuck with me. I can't help but think my soul needs to throw on a bikini and book the next flight out of here! Does your soul need a vacation, too?

It can be tough to get to know the real you when you are surrounded by noise and busyness. To deeply understand yourself and gain greater self-awareness, time alone is needed. Time to be alone, but not to be lonely. A chance to connect with yourself, enjoy your own company and be still.

When you're at the bottom of the confidence tree, when you're lost or precarious, you tend to fill your time with people and "stuff". You are busy, busy, busy. The problem is, if you keep yourself busy and remain focussed on other people, you can't focus on yourself. If you are always having conversations with other people, your self-talk can't be heard.

Sure, you can avoid issues. You can avoid thinking about yourself and your situation. You can pretend everything is peachy and carry on with life. I agree that in difficult times when you feel insecure and your confidence plummets, filling your calendar eases the pain in the short term. It keeps you occupied and out of a negative headspace. At my lowest confidence point, I filled every weekend with events: brunches with friends, coffee dates, huge nights out − anything to stop me from thinking about what was going on in my life and how I was feeling. But there comes a time when to move forward and rebuild your confidence, you need to focus on yourself and get to know you again.

As a leader, busyness can be all consuming. It's difficult to find the time to shut out the rest of the world, switch off from the pressures of your job and the needs of your team, and just be. Add to this the busyness of your home life − housework, errands, children, partner, pets − and it's no wonder solitude can feel like a pipe dream. But you need to find that time. You need to sit with yourself and spend some time just with you. Make it a priority. Leaders can spend so much time "doing" that they stop "being". One of your key responsibilities as a leader is to think and plan for the future. You need to create space to do this − "thinking" space without the noise and distractions.

Sometimes, being alone and having that one-on-one time with yourself is frightening. It can be confronting. You may want to avoid it at all costs. I know that when I avoid being alone, it's a sign of something else going on that I'm not ready to confront. I don't want to be alone because it means I can't escape the talk inside my head.

When I feel like this, I often think about my sister, Rell. Recently, Rell travelled to India by herself to attend textile workshops and purchase fabric for her design business. It was her first trip to India and she loved exploring the country and experiencing the culture. She would send me photographs of herself enjoying a meal, sightseeing and having a beer at a rooftop bar.

I look at these photos and think about my sister's travels, not only to India but to many other exotic destinations. I admire her self-sufficiency. My sister enjoys her own company. No one else is needed. She loves spending time alone and considers it a luxury. How awesome! It's something I've always admired in her and try to emulate.

When you don't find time to be by yourself, you miss out on discovering your deepest thoughts and feelings. The busyness of life takes over and you fall into bed each night exhausted, only to wake up the next morning to start the daily grind all over again – another busy day. You may want to spend time alone, but feel it's impossible to get that time. I have known leaders to hide in coffee shops or unoccupied offices, or even work from home for a morning, to grab some quiet time. For me, as a mum to young children, it was hard to find any solitude at all, even when going to the toilet! There can be so many demands on your time and energy.

It doesn't matter what you do or where you are, so long as your time alone gives you the chance to learn more about yourself. You need to give yourself the opportunity to be quiet and still. You are the most important person in your life. Enjoy your own company and find out how absolutely amazing you are!

TIPS TO HELP YOU FIND SOLITUDE

- Schedule it in. You need to make the time to be by yourself. Put it in your diary and make it a habit.

- Remove external distractions. Turn off your mobile phone, the television, your laptop and anything else that will distract you.

- Deliberately slow your pace and steady your mind. Stop thinking about your preoccupations and let your thoughts unfold.

- Find a place that brings you peace. Get out of the office and experience a change of scenery. Where is your happy place? Some people find being out in nature works. I'm a Gold Coast girl, so for me, there's nothing better than taking a walk along the beach and looking at the ocean to clear my mind.

- Engage in an activity can help. Some people like to meditate or exercise. Others like to journal.

There comes a time when the world gets quiet and the only thing left is your own heart. So you'd better learn the sound of it. Otherwise, you'll never understand what it's saying.

SARAH DESSEN

CHAPTER 3.6

Learn through reflection

Ask yourself the right questions

Reflection is a great way to get to know yourself. Routinely asking yourself questions builds your self-awareness and gives you a deeper sense of who you are and what you believe in. Your answers provide insight into how you can improve yourself and move towards your goals. There may be times when your answers surprise you and you think, "Wow! Where did that come from?" A real "a-ha" moment.

Thoughtful answers help you see situations differently. Your answers could change your attitude and the way you respond to a situation in the future. For example, if something went wrong in your day, perhaps you made a bad decision at work, a simple question such as, "What did I learn from today's decision?", turns a negative situation and into a positive one. Asking questions helps you view every situation as an opportunity to learn. It's easier for you to identify areas that need growth and development. Questions also allow you to examine the meaning of a situation and your response to it, so you can learn more about yourself.

Sometimes, though, instead of taking the time to reflect on your day, week or year, you want to start planning your next goal or adventure. You want to move forward. I agree that planning and looking forward are things you should invest a lot of time in, but your recent past behaviour and way of thinking can provide you with a wealth of knowledge about yourself. They give you vital lessons to take forward into the next chapter of your life.

You may feel like you don't have the time to stop and reflect, or perhaps you don't want to. It might be too painful to think about a tough situation or what you said or did in the heat of the moment. It can be embarrassing to replay the situation in your head. But if you ignore it and pretend it didn't happen, you miss the chance to learn from it. Sometimes, it might be necessary to give yourself some space before revisiting a past situation or reaction but don't ignore it. Just don't be too harsh on yourself.

The intention of self-reflection is not to be overly critical. It's not about judging yourself, but it's also not about blaming others or playing the victim. It's important to be insightful yet playful with your answers. Keep them light. Instead of wasting time dwelling on the past, acknowledge it and use it to move forward.

Author and life coach Tony Robbins refers to these types of questions as power questions. Robbins says, "Successful people ask better questions and, as a result, they get better answers." So, it's time to think about what questions you could ask yourself to get better answers – and better results.

US author and business coach Marshall Goldsmith also believes asking questions – or "triggers", as he calls them – is key to personal growth, awareness and the ability to effectively lead others. Goldsmith has a friend ring him each night to ask him a series of questions, such as: "Did you do your best today to set clear goals, preserve your client relationships or be grateful for what you have?" Marshall has done this for years and revises the questions depending on his priorities. He rates his efforts on a scale of one to 10 and ensures he's honest with himself. He calls these questions triggers because they are cues that move you forward in life, in the direction of beneficial change, particularly in a leadership role.

Asking yourself, "What did I learn today to be a better leader tomorrow?", will set you up for success. You will always be looking for ways to improve, learn and develop your attitude and skills. This behaviour, in turn, influences your people and you will create a culture of continuous self-improvement and a workplace of lifelong learners.

Leaders can easily get caught up in the fast pace of their work environment and don't take the necessary time out to stop and slow down. Sometimes great leadership takes consideration and restraint. As a leader, you need to regularly turn off the noise, reflect and find the calm amongst the chaos.

By making self-reflection a habit and asking yourself the right questions, you get clarity on what makes you happy, what brings you joy and what you could do differently in your leadership role. It also helps you detect your purpose, your legacy and what connects you with your values.

You could set yourself reflection questions for the day, the week and the end of the year. It's important to create a ritual that works for you and ask questions that align with your priorities and direction. Your questions should be framed positively and have a useful outcome. For example, asking, "Why don't I have the confidence to speak up at a meeting?" can be reframed as, "What can I do at the next meeting to be more confident to speak up?"

Sometimes your answers will come straight away; other times, they may take a little longer. You might find it useful to use the same set of questions for a period of time to gain clarity and a deeper understanding of a behaviour or attitude. Record your questions and answers, either on paper or digitally. It's useful to look back at what you wrote a year ago to remember where you have been and how far you have come.

So, sit back, put your feet up, and ask yourself the right questions for you at this time in your life. Make it a habit and you will gain deeper self-awareness and grow your confidence as a leader.

SELF-REFLECTION QUESTIONS

1. What did I learn today?

_____

_____

_____

2. What was the most important thing I did today?

_____

_____

_____

3. What do I need to let go of?

_____

_____

_____

4. What am I happy about in my life right now?

_____

_____

_____

5. What am I proud of?

_____

_____

_____

6. What am I grateful for?

_____

_____

_____

7. What do I enjoy doing most in my life?

_____

_____

_____

_____

8. What did I give to others today?

_____

_____

_____

_____

9. Who do I spend the most time with?

_____

_____

_____

10. Who makes me feel happy?

_____

_____

_____

11. What do I want to learn next?

_____

_____

_____

12. What am I making excuses for not doing?

_____

_____

_____

13. How can I be more helpful to others?

_____

_____

_____

14. What did I do for myself today?

_____

_____

_____

15. What can I accept that I can't change?

_____

_____

_____

_____

*Quality questions create
a quality life.*

ANTHONY ROBBINS

CHAPTER 3.7

Reduce your choices

Simplify your life

Choice is a privilege. It opens the door to a world of possibilities, giving you ownership of your destiny. Choice is empowering – but can there be such a thing as too much choice?

Choice is a double-edged sword. On the one hand, it allows us freedom and autonomy. On the other, it can overwhelm and paralyse. When you are at the bottom of the confidence tree, feeling lost or precarious and unsure of yourself, too much choice has a negative impact.

In so many aspects of our lives, we have unlimited choices. Not so long ago (as I keep telling my twenty-something-year-old girlfriends), if you wanted to meet a guy, you had to meet him *in person* – at a bar, at work or through a mutual friend. Now, you don't even need to leave your house – you can simply go online. The problem with online dating sites is that you can swipe for hours and still not choose a date. Your choice is endless.

It's the same with education. For parents who need to decide which school to send their children, there are so many choices. And it's the same at restaurants and bars. On weekends, when my girlfriends and I head out for a drink, I'm often handed a six-page wine list. I mean, really? Do we need that many options?

Too much choice can cloud your judgement. The unnecessary noise and distraction it creates causes you to feel overwhelmed. You may have had a clear idea of what you wanted, but when you're presented with so many choices, you start to doubt yourself. "Hang on a minute, is this really what I wanted?"

I'm not saying you should eliminate choice altogether, but you need to know when your options overwhelm you and make you feel anxious. You need to know when and how to simplify.

American psychologist Barry Schwartz, in his book *The Paradox of Choice – Why More is Less*, says that having too many choices can negatively impact well-being and happiness. In one study cited by Schwartz, researchers set up two displays of jams at a shopping centre. Shoppers could sample the jam and were given a $1 discount if they bought a jar of jam. In one display, there were six jams to choose from, and in the other, there were more than 24 jams. What do you think happened? Thirty percent of the people exposed to the small selection bought a jar of jam, but only three percent of people exposed to the larger selection made a purchase.

Have you ever had this experience, where too much choice left you unable to choose at all? I certainly have. There have been times when I've hit the shops on a Saturday afternoon, looking for the perfect outfit. I've gone into one of the huge department stores and wandered aimlessly around three floors of women's clothing. I have become frustrated and anxious, no longer having any idea of what I wanted. I have either come home with nothing and have had to wear something already in my wardrobe (the shame!) or I have come home with a completely inappropriate, uncomfortable outfit that's just not me.

Compare this to my experience shopping at one of my favourite boutiques. There, my choice is limited, there are only a couple of racks of clothing, but it's what I want. It's congruent with who I am and I know I'm going to be able to find something. My experience there is completely different to the big department store.

You can take this approach of simplification to all aspects of your life. Remember, less is more. As a leader, decision making is made easier when you simplify your life and limit your choices. It enables you to work more efficiently and cut through the noise. Your time is precious. When you know your personal values and beliefs, when you limit your choices to the ones that align with who you are and what you stand for as a leader, you save time and energy.

Choice can bring about so many positive opportunities for you as a leader and your organisation. Embrace it and use it. However, when choice starts to overwhelm you and impacts your judgement, it's time to step away. It's time to simplify.

TIPS TO SIMPLIFY YOUR CHOICES

- Know your values and beliefs.

- Connect your choices with those values and beliefs. For example, the type of work you accept, the people you engage with, the clients you work for, even where you do your shopping.

- Listen to your gut. What feels right? Don't ignore that.

- Reduce the noise in your life, particularly from your online community.

- Limit your interaction with people and organisations to the ones you truly connect with and gain value from.

The ability to simplify means to eliminate the unnecessary so that the necessary may speak.

HANS HOFMANN

CHAPTER 3.8

Focus on your priorities

Forget balance

How much do you try to balance in your life?

Do you try to be the best mum? The dedicated wife? A sex goddess in the bedroom? Do you focus on climbing the corporate ladder while trying to study on the side? Do you think about that master's degree and how it could make all the difference to your career?

Do you care for your aging parents? Does your girlfriend need your support through her messy divorce? Do you try to fit in a yoga class once a week, as well as the gym? Do you have to book a girls' weekend away six months in advance so you can find a "free" weekend that works for everyone?

Do you attend the school's trivia night and sign up for canteen roster at your son's football club? Do you attempt to keep the house perfect? Do you buy your mother-in-law's birthday present? Do you do a grocery run every second day? Get your nails done? Your hair? Waxing, tinting, threading? Do you ...

Argh! Enough! I don't know about you, but I'm exhausted. It's time to stop, take a breath and accept that you can't do everything and you can't be everything to everyone.

In June 2003, at 29 years of age, I was a senior lawyer in a law firm and a new mum. I had just given birth to my son, Tom. He arrived four weeks early on Friday the 13th, of all days. I was like most first-time mothers, overwhelmed by the changes this tiny new person brought to my life.

During this time, I was fiercely dedicated to becoming a partner in the law firm. I wanted it so badly, I dreamt about it. It was my career goal and I knew it was just around the corner if I worked hard enough.

When Tom was about four or five weeks old, a leadership retreat was booked at South Stradbroke Island. When I got the invitation, I thought, "There is no way I'm going to miss this event." I told my husband to pack everything, including our son (and there is a lot to pack up when it's your first born!), because we were heading to Stradbroke!

Eight years later, in 2011, my last child, Jack, was born. If someone had asked me then to pack up and attend a leadership retreat, I would have told them to get lost. Why? Because my priorities had changed. At this stage of my life, I had achieved partnership and was working part-time in the law firm, no longer doing file work but facilitating workshops and retreats as part of the learning and development team. My Mum had just passed away and my husband was going through an enormous amount of pressure at work. It was a time for me to focus on my family. A real shift of my priorities.

Even when I consider the past four years of my life, I have prioritised so many different things at different times. There have been times when my work was number one. There have been times when my children came first. I spent time caring for my Dad and making sure he was comfortable. Other times, my physical health was a major priority and I'd hit the gym three or four times a week to get that much-needed release of endorphins. Then there were times when I was on the dating scene and finding a partner was front of mind.

Have I ever found complete balance? No, never. Something is always more important than something else. As Quentin Bryce, former Governor-General of Australia, said: "For a very long time now, I've been saying to young women, you can have it all, but not all at the same time ... It's easier to be a workaholic than to have a truly balanced life. It's very tough for a lot of women teetering on that tightrope of balance and balancing too many responsibilities."

We need to step off that tightrope. It's exhausting. Forget about the pressure of obtaining balance in your life, because it doesn't exist. Just when you think you've got it right, something else will happen and send you into a spin. You might get an unexpected phone call from school about one of your kids, a major project will come up at work, a parent may suddenly fall ill or a friend might need your help.

Life is full of swings and roundabouts. Your priorities at every stage of life will change. It's what makes life interesting. You never know what's around the corner, so learn to embrace it. Let go of trying to find the perfect balance and ask yourself, "What are my priorities at this time of my life, based on my values and circumstances? What's going on for me right now?"

Think of life as a stage production. Not everyone or everything can be on stage at the same time. Each act and number has different cast members, props and stage settings. There is a focus and theme to each number. They are connected, each adding to the overall story, but they are different and have their own purpose. Your life is like that production.

Some aspects of your life will be backstage at certain times. They'll be in the wings, waiting patiently for their time in the spotlight. Other aspects will take centre stage. Then, things will change, and what was backstage will come to the fore.

You simply don't have the resources, time or energy to put every part of your life in the spotlight all the time. It would be absolutely exhausting. At some point, something has got to give. Stop feeling guilty about not being everything to everyone and not being able to fit everything in.

There's no need to be so hard on yourself. It's okay to put something to one side if you need to. Remember, it's just in the wings. I often remind myself of that when it comes to a work project or the gym. Instead of chastising myself, I think, "Okay, that's not a focus at this time, but it will be in the future." You can be light with it and let it go.

If balance is your goal and you never achieve it, you will always feel inadequate, you will never feel good enough. Your confidence will plummet as your guilt skyrockets. This is not the way for a leader to live. As a leader, you need to be clear on your top priorities and set clear goals for the upcoming week, month, quarter and year. Just like you, your people need to know where to put their attention and focus. Being clear on your priorities and expectations builds trust with your team members and sets them up to succeed.

When you let go of balance, life becomes simpler. You will see a real difference in your productivity and achievements, and experience a deeper level of self-awareness.

QUESTIONS TO START FOCUSING ON YOUR PRIORITIES

1. What are your current priorities based on your values and life situation?

_____

_____

_____

_____

2. Do you give these priorities the time, focus and attention they need?

_____

_____

_____

_____

3. What needs to take a back seat at this time to ensure your priorities come first?

_____

_____

_____

4. What actions do you need to take to make this happen?

_____

_____

_____

Focus on your burning priorities. Say no to everything else. Life's short. You only get one shot at great.

ROBIN SHARMA

CHAPTER 3.9

Try new things

Get out of your comfort zone

Your comfort zone is a beautiful place. It's where you feel secure and protected. But if you want to deeply understand yourself, there are times when you need to step out and take a risk. You must get comfortable with being uncomfortable.

There is a part of each of us that loves routine and pattern. In your comfort zone, there is little stress and little risk, but there is also less opportunity for you to get to know yourself. If you stick to your same routine, you'll only ever know one part of yourself. You won't know the full you, all your glorious dimensions.

New experiences bring out different responses. Sometimes, you need to challenge yourself and see what is revealed. Only then will you learn what you're truly capable of.

CHAPTER 3.9

There are times in your life when you do need the security of routine and certainty. Your comfort zone provides you with a much-needed stress-free zone. It also gives you the chance to process and reflect on your experiences. However, if you never step outside of it, you will struggle to grow. Opportunities will pass you by. At some point in your life, you will look back and think, "If only ..."

Neuroscience tells us we need to get out of our comfort zone to rewire our brain. It is possible to train your brain to respond to challenges in new and more effective ways. To do this, you need to experience new things.

A good friend of mine always asks, "What else is possible?" I love this question. Until you try, you don't know what else is possible. So, try something new. You may surprise yourself.

When I think about this concept of trying new things, I'm reminded of the theme song of the US sitcom Cheers. Do you remember this song? (Or am I just showing my age?)

> *Sometimes you wanna go where everybody knows your name, and they're always glad you came.*
> *You wanna be where you can see our troubles are all the same.*
> *You wanna be where everybody knows your name.*

During my life, it seems like I've spent a long time at that *Cheers* bar. A place where everyone was glad I came, our troubles were all the same, and everybody knew my name. I was happy, but there was that niggle. I felt there was something different, something more I could be doing, and I knew I wouldn't discover what that was if I stayed in the same place. I knew stepping out of my comfort zone would be frightening, but I also knew it was going to be completely exhilarating. It's scary to go where people don't know your name and may not even care that you came. But it's in that space where you just might discover a part of yourself you didn't know existed.

I remember one night, I was umming and ahhing about whether to go to a Business Chicks event on the Gold Coast. I wouldn't know anyone there. What would it be like? Then it started to rain. And it was cold. But I thought to myself, nothing ventured, nothing gained, so I got dressed and headed out.

I walked into the event and introduced myself to a number of women. I said, "Hey. I'm Midja. Thank you for your smiling faces because I was really nervous walking in here tonight!" One woman said, "Yes, me too. I nearly didn't come." Then another woman said, "I only came because my friend said she would come with me." We all had a giggle. You see, often the way you're feeling is the way others feel, too.

Try to reframe your thinking about new situations and experiences. Instead of feeling nervous about them, feel excited. Of course, I love it when I go to an event and people turn around and say, "Hey Midja!" It makes me feel all warm and fuzzy and I need some of that in my life. I think you do, too. However, I also need to get out there and meet new people – people who don't know my name, my history or my background. People who have no preconceived ideas of who I am and what I do. It's these people who will challenge me and possibly make me see myself differently.

If you are willing to stretch yourself and take risks as a leader, you will expand your influence and discover what you're truly capable of achieving. You will develop new skills and capabilities to face even greater challenges in the future. Leadership is not about standing still and accepting the status quo. It's about improvement, innovation, exploration and, at times, pushing the boundaries.

Stepping outside your comfort zone can feel awkward and uncomfortable. But outside your comfort zone is a place of great opportunity. So, step outside and find out how much you can grow and learn about yourself.

IDEAS TO STEP OUTSIDE OF YOUR COMFORT ZONE

1. Deliberately do the opposite of what you would normally do.

2. Meet new people outside your industry.

3. Do an extreme challenge.

4. Learn a musical instrument.

5. Volunteer.

6. Book a holiday to somewhere new.

7. Take a fun class – ever tried tap dancing?

8. Try a new recipe in the kitchen.

9. Rock up to an event where you don't know anyone.

10. Take a different route to work.

11. Read a book or watch a TED talk about something you know nothing about.

12. Learn a new language.

13. Become a mentor.

14. Get out in nature.

15. Change your appearance.

16. Take up a new project at work.

17. Talk to a stranger.

Life is either a daring adventure or nothing at all.

HELEN KELLER

CHAPTER 3.10

Reboot your life

Time to break the circuit

Have you ever called IT support and reported a problem with your laptop, phone or iPad? What's the first piece of advice the tech guys always give you? They tell you to switch it off, wait, then switch it back on. Following this simple set of instructions fixes 99% of problems.

Life is the same. Sometimes, what I call a "life reboot" is just what you need. The only thing that is going to fix what's going on in your life is to turn off, wait, and turn back on.

There will be times in your life when you feel stuck. You may feel like you're caught between phases of your life. You can't move forward, but you also don't want to move backwards. You feel unsure of yourself and what your next move should be.

CHAPTER 3.10

It might be that your values, beliefs and, therefore, your view of the world has changed dramatically. Why, when and how many times this happens is different for everyone. It can rock you to your very core. It could be caused by a relationship breakdown, redundancy at work, the death of a loved one, the end of study, the birth of a child or any other significant event.

For me, 2016 marked a life reboot when my career and personal relationships changed significantly. I felt like I didn't know who I was anymore. I lost my sense of identity and didn't know what mattered to me.

My life reboot coincided with the midpoint of my life, my early 40s. I hate the phrase "mid-life crisis", but for some people that is an accurate description. They are in crisis mode. It's the realisation half your life is over, so you feel like it's now or never. It's a pivotal time when you can decide to either make a significant change in your life or stay on the same trajectory.

Up until this midlife point, you may have been busy chasing down a whole list of goals or achievements: marriage — tick, children — tick, career — tick, extra study — tick, circle of friends — tick, volunteer work — tick. You've been so focussed on these goals that when you find you've ticked all the boxes and there's nothing left on your list, you turn around and say, "Hang on a minute. Who am I again? What did I really want in life? What is there left for me to do?" You had always imagined that once you'd ticked all the boxes, you would arrive at some magical place in your life where you were happy and fulfilled, but sadly, you're not.

In fact, research shows a consistent U-bend in life when it comes to levels of happiness. People are least happy in their 40s and early 50s. We reach our lowest level of happiness at a global average of

46 years. Sorry to get all doom and gloom on you, that's not my intention. It's just a way of showing you that if you're feeling like this, it's perfectly normal and your feelings are shared by many others. Want to know the good news? At 70, you'll be as happy as you were at 20![1]

No matter when this feeling creeps up on you, it can feel like you're stuck in quicksand. That's how I felt. I couldn't turn back but I couldn't lift my legs to move forward, either. Then, after being stuck for a while, there is the sensation of sinking. You feel you're going under. It may be a slow descent, but if you keep sinking you will disappear and lose yourself. This is the time when you need to act and pull yourself out.

It can be a time of restlessness, anxiety and discontentment. You look in the mirror and the person staring back at you is a stranger. You hardly recognise yourself. The old you has gone, but you haven't figured out who the new you is yet.

The people closest to you may not understand how you're feeling and may not know how to help you. They may not even want to. Change can be scary and confronting. To your family and friends, you look the same and sound the same, but you know something has shifted. You are not the same. You have a choice: do nothing and sink, or do a life reboot.

If you don't break the circuit, you'll keep getting the same error messages and the same repeated behaviour. Certain attitudes and behaviours create patterns in your life. At some point, you realise these attitudes and behaviours aren't working. You need to jolt yourself out of complacency so you can think differently and create the positive change needed to get out of the quicksand.

---

1 "The U-bend of life." *The Economist*, 16 December, 2010.

CHAPTER 3.10

When you feel like this, you are most likely at the bottom of the confidence tree, at least in some aspect of your life or with an important relationship. You feel precarious and you lack clarity and confidence.

A reboot gives you the chance to focus on what we've discussed in this chapter: getting to know yourself again. This is your chance to explore, to get away, to try new things, to act differently and to question yourself and where you want to go. Be warned: it might be a highly frustrating time. It will take a lot of hard work and you will feel uncomfortable but stay with it. Remember, you need to be comfortable with being uncomfortable. These feelings of uncertainty and restlessness will not last forever.

How long does a reboot take? You know what I'm going to say. It takes as long as it takes. Frustrating, right? Yes, but it can't be rushed.

Once you've rebooted, once you've done the work on getting to know yourself, the roots of your confidence tree are firmly in place. The most important thing now is to switch yourself back on and show yourself to the world. When version 2.0 (or whatever version you are up to) is ready, don't be hard on yourself about how long the process has taken. Don't dwell on the choices and decisions you've made along the way. I know some of the choices I made during my life reboot are cringe-worthy – just ask my friends! But you know what? My choices were all part of the experience and they got me to where I am now.

Your reboot is a defining time in your life. It's a moment when things will never be the same again. Your life is divided into two parts: before this happened and after this happened.

Your reboot might be difficult and challenging, but it will be worth it when you turn back on with clarity and purpose, knowing exactly who you are!

TIPS TO REMEMBER DURING THE LIFE REBOOT

- What you're feeling is normal. Relax. It's an exciting time of personal growth and opportunity.

- Consider your values and your legacy.

- Ask yourself the tough questions, reflect on where you've been and where you want to go, and examine your current beliefs and your story so far.

- Give yourself the time and space you need to rediscover yourself.

- Be kind to yourself and don't feel guilty about focussing on you.

- Give yourself a break from the everyday tasks if you can, even if it's just for a short while.

- Don't rush it. It takes as long as it takes.

Twenty years from now you will
be more disappointed by the things
that you didn't do than by the
ones you did do. So throw off the
bowlines. Sail away from the
harbour. Catch the trade winds
in your sails. Explore. Dream.
Discover.

MARK TWAIN

CHAPTER 4

BE YOURSELF

CHAPTER 4

Be yourself

"I can't think of any better representation of beauty than someone who is unafraid to be herself."

– EMMA STONE

It's time for you to be beautiful!

Now that you've done the work on knowing yourself, it's time to show yourself to the world. There's no point doing all that work on yourself if you don't let others see you and get to know the real you.

Your confidence level is now steady. You know yourself, but you haven't had the opportunity or the courage to show yourself. You don't feel you have a voice yet.

One Saturday morning in August 1997, I was sitting at the kitchen table at my Mum and Dad's house looking at the job ads in the newspaper. (Yes, it was back in the day of no internet, so Brisbane's *Courier Mail* newspaper was the place to find a job – there was no

CHAPTER 4

SEEK or LinkedIn). I was lucky enough to stumble across a job ad for an articled clerk of a law firm. I applied for the job, not knowing anything about the firm or what they did. I didn't know anyone who worked there. In fact, I didn't even know what it was like to be a lawyer and had no idea what a typical day was like. So, it was by luck, some divine force, destiny or whatever you want to call it that I landed this job.

After resigning from my previous job with Pricewaterhouse Urwick and moving back in with Mum and Dad, I'm sure my parents were as happy as I was that I got that job. Little did I know that it was the start of a wonderful 19-year relationship.

The most amazing thing about that firm, apart from the awesome people I met and got to work with and who are still my besties, was that every day I got to be me. In all my uniqueness and craziness, they accepted me. More than that, they valued me. What a gift to be given!

When you can be yourself, your true authentic self, it is so liberating. You don't need to fear being judged. You can focus on doing your very best work and the difference you can make in the world. You can be free in your authenticity. There is no internal conflict.

It is this authenticity that is the key to great leadership. As a leader, the most important thing you can do is make a connection with your people. People are not going to follow you if they don't know you. They won't trust you and they won't commit to you. To build trust as a leader, your people need to hear your story and know what you stand for. They need to get to know the real you. This means building a leadership brand that is authentic and based on everything you discovered about yourself in Chapter 3.

You may feel that you can't be yourself because others will judge you and not accept you for who you are. I say, try. Give it a shot. Be yourself and see what happens. In the words of Dr Seuss, "Be who you are and say what you feel because those who mind don't matter and those who matter don't mind." You don't have to make any apologies for being yourself.

When you can't be yourself, it's exhausting. You bottle everything up. It's like trying to hold a beach ball under the water – you can't do it forever. One day, you'll lose your grip on that beach ball and it's going to pop up and smack you in the face. Think of all that time and energy you expend, pretending to be someone you're not. All that time feeling frustrated because deep down, you knew who you were but you didn't show it.

In this chapter, you will discover how you can:

- Amplify your strengths
- Be present
- Let go of perfection
- Make a decision
- Own your time
- Tell your story
- Put yourself first
- Stop reacting
- Take off your armour
- Create your brand

*Being yourself can be a revolutionary act.
In a world that wants us to whisper, I choose to yell.*

LUVVIE AJAYI

CHAPTER 4.1

Amplify your strengths

Become extraordinary at something

When I open my eyes each morning, a message stares back at me in a white frame with beautiful gold writing. It says, "You did not wake up today to be mediocre." Each morning, I read that message and say to myself, "No, you did not." And neither did you.

Leaders often ask me, "Should I spend my time focussing on my strengths, the things I'm already good at? Or should I try to improve my weaknesses, the gaps in my skills?" My answer is to always play to your strengths.

To me, it comes down to this. **You can either be ordinary at everything or be extraordinary at something.** If you focus on your weaknesses, you may become well rounded. People often think that's a great thing. They put their energy and focus on improving their weaknesses to be a jack of all trades and increase their overall skills. However, you must ask yourself, "Do I want to be described as well-rounded or extraordinary?" I know which one I want to be.

If you play to your strengths, you can become extraordinary. The most inspiring leaders are known for something. They know their ace card and they know how to use it. They make sure they play to their strengths because they know that in doing so, they make the biggest difference to the lives of others.

In the previous chapter, Know Yourself, we spoke about finding your magic, your talent, and your gift to the world. Now it is time to focus on it. You need to give it all the energy it deserves. You must amplify it and dial it up. I'm talking high definition!

Of course, you need to be aware of your weaknesses and we'll talk about those later in this chapter, but you don't want to waste time on them.

Malcolm Gladwell, in his book *Outliers*, refers to the 10,000-hour rule, based on the research of Herbert Simon and William Chase. According to this rule, it takes 10,000 hours – in other words, a lot of time and practice – to become proficient at a complex task.

If it takes that much time and effort to become exceptional at something, don't waste it by focussing on things that will make you mediocre or average. Keep the spotlight on your strengths, where you are centre stage and where you shine. When you play to your strengths, you take the lead. Why would you step away from centre stage to make room for something you're not good at, something you don't enjoy and doesn't come naturally? The spotlight shines brightest when you're doing your best work, the work you're meant to do, and contributing in the most meaningful way possible.

At a young age, I knew I loved to talk. I remember the joy that came from my show-and-tell days at school. It was my favourite time of the week. While my friends dreaded getting up in front of the class, I was nearly wetting my pants with excitement. This love of presenting stayed with me and grew.

When I was a lawyer, I took every opportunity to present anything at any time to anyone. In addition to managing a law office and servicing my clients, I would facilitate, train and present. I was part of the learning and development team, without officially being part of the team. I presented at team meetings, firm strategy days, Law Association days, induction courses, anything. Why? Because I wanted to get to that 10,000 hours of facilitating and speaking. I knew it wasn't going to happen by accident. I had to be deliberate about it.

In other words, if you don't actively seek opportunities to amplify your strengths, you'll never fully discover what you're capable of. Imagine what's possible if you stopped focussing on your weaknesses and gave your full focus to strengthening your magic, your gift. Think about what you could achieve.

The great news is you have more resources at your fingertips than ever before to practice and hone your talent: online courses, TED Talks, public workshops, podcasts, research papers, YouTube clips, the list goes on.

A mentor is another highly valuable option. A mentor is someone you aspire to be in your field of expertise. They've been there, done that and bought the T-shirt! They are someone who's inspiring and extremely knowledgeable in your area of proficiency. You can learn a lot from your mistakes but you can learn a lot more from the mistakes of a mentor. My own mentor has been an amazing source of knowledge and motivation. Who do you admire and aspire to be? Follow them on social media, reach out to them and ask whether they would be willing to take you under their wing.

Remember, the greatest impact comes from amplifying your talent. As a leader, when you use your strengths to make a difference in the lives of others, they'll forgive you your weaknesses. In fact, they may not even notice them.

So, give your strengths your full focus and attention. Give 100%. I say if you're going to do something, do it big. Go the whole way. Don't settle for good enough or mediocre – strive to be extraordinary.

QUESTIONS TO HELP YOU AMPLIFY YOUR STRENGTHS

1. Firstly, what are your strengths? (from Chapter 3: Know Yourself)

    _____

    _____

    _____

    _____

    _____

2. What do you currently do to develop your strengths?

    _____

    _____

    _____

    _____

3. How much time per week do you invest in developing them?

    _____

    _____

    _____

    _____

4. What further opportunities can you explore to play to your strengths?

_____

_____

_____

_____

_____

5. Do you have a mentor or coach to challenge you and hold you accountable?

_____

_____

_____

_____

_____

Focussing on strengths is the surest way to greater job satisfaction, team performance and organisational excellence.

MARCUS BUCKINGHAM

CHAPTER 4.2

Be present

Savour the moment

In her memoir, *Eat Pray Love*, author Elizabeth Gilbert writes about a friend who would exclaim whenever she saw a beautiful place, "It's so beautiful here. I want to come back here someday."

"It takes all my persuasive powers," Gilbert says, "to try to convince her that she is already here."

There are times when we get so caught up in the past or future, we neglect what is going on right now.

There is nothing you can do about what has been. It's in the past. There is value in acknowledging your experiences and learning from them, as we've already explored. But excessive deliberation on the past is futile. There is no going back and no changing what has been. So, accept the past, forgive yourself (and others, if you need to) and be fully present today. *Do not let yesterday hold today ransom.*

Similarly, worrying about the future can impact your joy in the present. Worrying doesn't take away tomorrow's troubles. It simply takes away today's peace. It's necessary to plan and set goals but don't become so overwhelmed by the "what ifs" that you can't enjoy today. As writer Mark Twain said, "I have known a great many troubles, but most of them never happened." How much time and energy have you spent worrying about something that never came to fruition? Your worries, doubts and stress often come from the past or the future – rarely from the present.

To me, being present is like that feeling you get under water. There is that great sensation when you are in the surf, pool or even in the bath when your ears are blocked, there's no noise and you're just with yourself.

My youngest son, Jack, has always loved that feeling. Even as a toddler, he loved nothing more than lying in the bath, covered in water with only his eyes, nose and mouth uncovered. Peaceful, no distractions, hearing only his breathing. Being right there in the moment.

To be an authentic leader, to influence others and create meaningful relationships, you need to be present and lead in the moment. Your people need your full attention and they deserve it. It is impossible to influence others when they don't feel listened to or understood. One of the partners of the law firm I worked at told me that when someone came into her office, her automatic response was to stop typing, turn towards them and smile. I love that.

If you're distracted and not fully present as a leader, you will miss opportunities to connect with your people. In your haste to move on to the next conversation or meeting, you might make commitments and promises you can't deliver. "That report, sure, I'll have a read of it today. Friday's meeting – yes, I'll be there. Approval for that training session – consider it done." Busy, busy, busy. Making promises and setting expectations. All good, right? It's only good if you follow through.

Keeping promises is one of the most important things you can do as a leader. Often when you make a promise, your intention is to follow it through, but then you get so busy and distracted and you let the promise go. You think, "Ah well, it was only something small, I'll get around to it. I'm sure they will understand how busy I am." No! They will remember your broken promise. It was a big deal to them and they were counting on you. That's why it's so important to slow down, be present with your people and consider the impact before you make a promise.

Now, I'm not saying this is easy. It can be tough, particularly in this age of distraction. Our work lives are becoming more and more blurred with our home lives. There doesn't seem to be a clear-cut distinction between them anymore. You have your mobile phone, laptop, smartwatch, Snapchats, Facebook messages, Tweets, emails, texts, the list goes on. No wonder it's tough to focus on what is happening right in front of you.

I'm sure you've been to a restaurant and glanced around the tables. What do you see? People sitting across from people (like, real people in the flesh), but instead of engaging with them, they're on their phone engaging with their screen. Have you ever been guilty of this? I know I have.

CHAPTER 4.2

Technology can be a beautiful thing. It connects us, engages us and opens a world of opportunities. However, it's by no means a substitute for real human contact and experience.

I can't remember when it happened, but at some point during my career as a lawyer, it became acceptable to take your mobile phone to a meeting and put it on the table. I can recall the first time it happened and how it made me feel. I felt like I was less important and what I said didn't matter. I didn't feel valued.

As a leader, I'm sure that's not how you want to make your people feel. The constant connection with our tech devices has become a habit. It stops us from being ourselves and being truly present with the people in front of us.

So, how can you become more present?

- Be aware of your technology use. Stop taking your phone to meetings, restaurants and social occasions.

- Practices like meditation, mindfulness and embodiment can help develop your capacity to be fully present.

- Slow down and savour the moment. Relish and luxuriate in whatever you're doing. This means using all your senses. In one study, participants were instructed to savour two pleasurable experiences a day and reflect on each for a few minutes. The researchers found that regular savouring significantly increased happiness and reduced negative feelings in participants.[1] One of my girlfriends, Louise, asked me, "How do you think we can slow down time? Life just seems to be going past so quickly." I think the practice of

1 Lyubomirsky, S. *The How of Happiness*. Penguin Putnam, New York, 2009.

savouring the moment is a step in the right direction. Not only will you feel happier and experience more joy, you'll be less stressed. It will allow you to be you, to be more authentic and genuine.

Right here, right now is all you have, so pay attention to it. Embrace the present with gratefulness. Don't live out of your memories or dreams, or you'll miss out on what is happening right now.

HOW PRESENT ARE YOU?

- Do you find yourself checking your emails/messages while talking to others?

- Do you take your phone into meetings and restaurants – in fact, everywhere?

- Do you try to do two or three (or more) things at once?

- Do you ever eat while standing up or working at your desk?

- Do you find yourself interrupting people to move the conversation along?

- During a conversation, do you find your thoughts wandering and do you have to ask people to repeat what they just said?

- Do you listen with the intent to fully understand or just to reply?

- Do you take any time out during your day to stop "doing" and just "be"?

_____

_____

_____

_____

Quit, don't quit. Noodles, don't noodles. You are too concerned with what was and with what will be. Yesterday is history, tomorrow is a mystery, but today is a gift. That is why it is called the present.

MASTER OOGWAY, KUNG FU PANDA

CHAPTER 4.3

Let go of perfection

Acknowledge your flaws

I'm not perfect and guess what? You aren't either. Thank goodness! But did you know that nearly eight in 10 women feel some pressure to never make mistakes or show weakness?[1] That's some serious stress and anxiety! As women, we bear the burden of perfectionism and it's a real confidence killer.

Letting go of the idea that you should be great at everything is liberating. Perfectionism is an impossible goal, just like the balance we spoke about in Chapter 3. It's a construct, a script you have read and memorised, a fiction about what you supposedly need to do to succeed and be enough in this world. You might have a script in your head about what it means to be the perfect wife, mother,

1 Moss, R. "Women's Body Confidence Is A 'Critical Issue' Worldwide, Warns Dove's Largest Ever Report." *Huffington Post*, 21 June, 2016. http://www.huffingtonpost.co.uk/entry/dove-global-body-image-report_uk_5762a6a1e4b0681487dcc470

daughter, friend and leader. You fixate on your performance at home, university, work, yoga class and even on holiday. It's never-ending.

But the truth is no one can be great at everything. Everyone has weaknesses, even the greatest and most successful leaders. You cannot be everything to everyone. Being yourself is about amplifying your strengths and acknowledging your weaknesses and flaws. You don't want to dwell on them, but it's important you acknowledge them, be real about them and decide how to deal with them.

As a leader, mother and friend, when you stop striving for perfection and say to others honestly, "I actually suck at these things over here and I'm OK with that," it gives them permission to stop judging themselves so harshly. They, too, can take a deep breath and stop striving for perfection. You create a new way for them to measure success and know what it means to be enough. They no longer fear admitting their flaws, they feel safer taking a risk and know it's OK if they fail. What a gift you can give others: permission to throw out the perfection script!

Acknowledging your weaknesses means you can be comfortable in your own skin. You get to be the real you because you're being honest and truthful with yourself. Your weaknesses humanise you, which means you are more approachable as a leader. Yes, we want leaders to be confident, but real confidence comes from within. Confidence comes from knowing who you are and having a strong, unwavering self-belief. It doesn't come from being perfect or pretending to be perfect. In fact, if someone seems too perfect at everything, it can create suspicion. Can you really trust someone who is that perfect? It seems too good to be true and you start to question them. "Is there something they're hiding?"

Great leadership is letting go of the need to be right and to know more than everyone else. It's not about being the best at everything. Leadership is being confident enough to ask for help. Your weaknesses are someone else's strengths, and a great leader knows when they need to acknowledge and rely on other people's expertise and knowledge. This, in turn, builds the confidence and skills of those around you.

You may be hesitant to admit to your weaknesses and your flaws, especially out loud. It might be tough for you to ask for help and to admit when you don't know something. You may have been told not to let your guard down as a leader, don't let them smell your weakness. How crazy is that?

Above all, leadership is about human connection. It's true, it's not easy to admit to your flaws in the workplace – it takes courage and a degree of vulnerability. But it is worth the risk. You'll create a strong bond with your people and gain a deep commitment from them. Your strengths will give them such value and inspiration they will forgive your faults or may not even notice them.

If you don't acknowledge your weaknesses, if you try to do everything, you may end up doing nothing at all. You will fail to meet deadlines because everything takes more time than it should. You then start feeling like a failure. In your quest for perfection, instead of looking flawless, you'll end up appearing incompetent to others and worse, you won't achieve your goals.

So, what can you do about your flaws and weaknesses?

Firstly, discover what they are. Hopefully, you have been blessed with some honest feedback from others in your career. If you haven't, seek it. Ask a trusted colleague for their feedback and explain why you want to know. As a leader, feedback from your manager and peers is always a gift. Hopefully, most of what you hear will not be a great surprise to you, but occasionally you will receive feedback that makes you step back and rethink your behaviour and its impact.

You can also gain an insight into your weaknesses by asking yourself questions: What challenges you at work? What do you put off until the last minute? Where do mistakes occur in your work and why has something failed in the past?

Once you know your weaknesses, acknowledge them, change your mindset about them and realise that even your weaknesses contribute to the amazing person you are. Your limitations make room for your talents. Don't dwell on them. Remember, you want to put your energy into your strengths.

When you consider your weakness, ask yourself: Do I have an opposite strength I can build upon? You see, for every strength, there is often an opposite weakness. We all have this dichotomy. Steve Jobs said that "in most cases, strengths and weaknesses are two sides of the same coin. A strength in one situation is a weakness in another yet the person can't switch gears." For example, a leader who has great vision and can see the bigger picture may have a lack of attention to detail. A leader who has an amazing ability to weigh up a situation and analyse a problem may have a pessimistic outlook. For many female leaders, a real strength is the ability to show empathy and make a strong emotional connection with their people. But along with that strength can be the weakness of rescuing their people when times get tough and wanting harmony in the team at any cost.

When a task requires a skill that is a weakness, ask yourself: Can it be delegated? Remember, your weakness may be someone else's strength.

If it can't be delegated, have some tools handy to help you and be disciplined. For example, being organised may not be your strong point, so ensure you take advantage of your calendar, reminder lists and spreadsheets. You may struggle with presentations at meetings, so you need to take the time to rehearse what you're going to say, make detailed notes and tell a story first to relax your nerves.

The best approach is to just get in and get it done. It's like being a child again, pushing that dreaded piece of broccoli around your dinner plate. If you eat it first, then you can move on and eat everything else. So, if you know there's a job that needs to be done that day or week and it isn't your forte, do it first and get it over with.

Let go of the need to be perfect. Be your true authentic self. **Your weaknesses, flaws and faults are part of who you are. And you are amazing.**

Every moment spent in a quest for impossible perfection is a missed opportunity to gift the world with your light, your presence and your love.

TO GAIN AN INSIGHT INTO YOUR LEVEL OF PERFECTIONISM AS A LEADER, ASK YOURSELF:

- Do you have an all-or-nothing approach? Do you either do everything well or don't do it at all?

- Do you find yourself criticising others for not doing things "right"?

- Do you have a highly specific manner in which things should be done in your team?

- Do you try to hide your weaknesses from others?

- Do you find it difficult to admit you don't know something and to ask for help?

- Do you avoid situations that might be fun but might make you look foolish or incompetent?

- Does your need to get things done correctly interfere with your relationships?

_____

_____

_____

_____

_____

*You are magnificent
beyond measure,
perfect in your imperfections,
and wonderfully made.*

ABIOLA ABRAMS

CHAPTER 4.4

Make a decision

Take responsibility

You're the decision maker in your life. To be authentic and live the life you want, you must make your own decisions and own the outcomes: the good, the bad and the ugly.

I wouldn't call myself a huge superhero fan but I do love the advice given by Uncle Ben to Spiderman: "With great power comes great responsibility." You have the ultimate power. You get to make every decision in your life, but with that comes a great deal of responsibility.

It is this responsibility that can make deferring decisions to others attractive. The "upside" of deferring decisions is that you get to come up with your own BEDtime story: Blame, Excuses, Denial. You can say to yourself, "I haven't been able to achieve what I wanted. I'm not happy or fulfilled. I can't really be myself because ... " (insert your BEDtime story here).

It might be a story of **blame**. The blame game is one of the greatest games on earth! If it's not the government's fault, it's the fault of your parents, your kids, your partner, your boss, your team members, your dog or the weather. The list goes on. There can be so many people and circumstances to point the finger at that you can sit back, not take responsibility and play the victim, which for some people feels good.

You can come up with a million **excuses** why you don't have the life you want. I had a mentor say to me once that you have one of two things in life: results or reasons. In other words, you either have what you want in your life or you have all the reasons why you don't. Of course, some excuses are valid. We all know bad stuff happens to good people all time. However, confident people take responsibility for the good and the bad and move forward. You need to ask yourself, do you want your life to be a result of your conditions, your past and your circumstances? Or do you want it to be a result of your choices?

You can also go into **denial** about your life and situation. It can feel safe to deny everything, bury your head in the sand and pretend things haven't happened or that you don't feel the way you do.

You may have some valid reasons for wanting to back away from decision making. It may be that you want to please others. You don't want to upset the people closest to you, so you put their needs before your own. It may also be that you don't know yourself well enough to make a decision. You don't feel confident making choices in your life because you don't know what you want. You think other people know you better, so whatever they decide will be for the best. You just follow along and do what other people do. Of course, it's great to learn from others and their journey, but you need to put it in the context of your own life, your own values, and your own beliefs and goals.

Perhaps you just don't **want** to take responsibility. It's easier and safer to let other people decide, then you can pull out that BEDtime story. If you don't make your own decisions, there will be people in your life who will be quick to make them for you. People who think they know best. They will jump at the chance. It might be a team member, your manager, your partner or your parents. The problem is, only *you* can know the real you. They may have your best interests at heart, they may think "this is what you want", but they base this on their own life experience and values – not yours.

If you allow other people to make choices in your life, at some point you may resent them for steering you in the wrong direction. You need to get into the driver's seat. Don't be a passenger in your life, because what do passengers do?

- They spend their time looking out the window. Do you feel sometimes that you're an observer in your own life?

- They whine about how long the journey is taking: "Are we there yet?" With no responsibility, they have no control over the timeframe.

- They fall asleep in the car, then wake up and think, "How did I get here? Where am I?" Have you ever felt like this? A week, a year or five years go by and you think to yourself, "How did I end up living this life and making these decisions?"

- They are preoccupied with the little details, like what music to play and what snacks to eat along the way. The big picture gets lost amongst the small stuff. The small stuff does have its place, but you should only focus on it once you've worked out the big questions, like where you're going, what route you're going to take and when you want to get there.

It's the driver who has ultimate control. Sure, they can be guided by others, they can take advice and get directions, but they're the ones who have control and steer the car in the right direction.

As a leader, one of the most powerful attributes you can model for your people is accountability. I often hear leaders say they want their people to be more accountable and take more responsibility. This attitude starts with you. You must create the culture you want by modelling it yourself.

As a leader, it is important you spend most of your time in the coaching space, asking questions, but there will be times when the decisions are up to you and you will need to make the call. This usually happens in tough times when you're needed the most. There may be consequences but you must stand up and make your decision. Trust in yourself, follow your beliefs and remember your values. And in the end, if you do make the wrong decision, own it. After all, you made that decision with the best of intentions and the best information you had at the time.

THE WINDOW AND THE MIRROR

I love the window and mirror metaphor for leadership. It goes like this: When things are going well in the team and goals are being met, a great leader looks out the window and acknowledges the contribution of their people. When things aren't going well and there are problems in the team, instead of looking out the window, a great leader will look in the mirror and take responsibility for the results.

Decisiveness is an important attribute for a leader. People will look up to you for guidance and inspiration. You want to be confident as a leader, strong and reliable – not a tree swaying in the breeze with shallow roots.

TIPS FOR EFFECTIVE DECISION MAKING

- Have the attitude that everything is a choice. You are the driver of your life, so get in the driver's seat!

- Don't let other people make decisions for you. If this is tough, start with some small things in your life and build up to the major decisions.

- When there is a fork in the road or if a decision could have major consequences, create some space. The old saying "sleep on it" is a good one.

- Base your decisions on who you are, your values, your beliefs, your goals and your legacy.

- If you end up making a "bad" decision, accept it and own it. Don't get out your BEDtime story and blame, make excuses or deny. Ask yourself, "What would I do differently next time and what did I learn?" Seek feedback from others and apologise if you need to.

I need to take an emotional breath, step back, and remind myself who's actually in charge of my life.

JUDITH KNOWLTON

CHAPTER 4.5

Own
your time

When to say yes and when to say no

"How are you?" The answer to that question used to be, "Well, thanks." But now when you ask it, often the response is one word: "Busy."

So, how busy are you? Is your busyness making you happy? Is it leading to a more fulfilling and meaningful life or just the opposite? If I ran into you on a Friday and asked what your top three achievements for the week were, would you be able to tell me?

You have no control over the amount of time you have in your day. I've heard time described as an equal opportunity employer: each of us has the same number of hours and minutes every day. Your power lies in what you choose to do with those hours and minutes. You have the power to choose what you say yes and what you say no to. This choice becomes much easier when you understand who you are and what your purpose is. Without knowing yourself, you will be at the mercy of others' urgent priorities.

You may find yourself saying yes to everyone and everything. You have built a strong reputation as someone who says yes. A lot of people rely on you. At some level, they have learnt if they keep asking you to do things, you will keep saying yes, so they keep targeting you and asking you to do one more thing. You've trained them how to treat you. But now it's time to take back control. This is your time and you won't get it back.

Keep in mind that when you say yes to something or someone in front of you, you say no to something or someone else. For example, if you say yes to coffee with a colleague, you say no to that webinar you were going to attend. If it's a yes to a networking evening, it's a no to dinner with your partner. Before saying yes, ask yourself: "If I say yes now, what am I saying no to? How does that sit with me? How does it feel?"

Saying yes might come from a good intention. You may have built your self-esteem and confidence on pleasing others. The problem is, you get lost in other people's priorities and expectations. When you say yes to things that don't add meaning or value to your life, it leaves you with no time to pursue the things you want. You can end up exhausted and feel as though you haven't achieved anything.

The drag on your time and energy becomes amplified as you move into a leadership position with more and more people wanting a piece of you, asking you just one more "quick question". You also end up being invited to more and more meetings. The more you accept, the heavier the load on your shoulders, and you lose sight of what's important. Your time is so valuable. You need to make smart decisions about where you spend it. Effective time management is not about fitting more things in. I don't think any of us want to be doing any *more*. We want to be doing less. We want to be able to focus on the people, the work and the experiences that mean something to us.

The secret to effective time management was something we explored in Chapter 3 – getting to know yourself and becoming crystal clear on who you are and what you want. Once you do that, you can be yourself. You can be authentic and real, which means you need to spend time on the things that will ensure you live by your values, achieve your goals and leave your legacy. Those are the things that matter most.

Being truly authentic means that you put your money where your mouth is. This is something not everyone does. For example, when you ask someone, "What do you value?", they might say, "Family." However, when you really look at where they spend their time, you discover that they spend little or no time with their significant other or children. Another person might answer that they value their health and physical well-being, but they haven't committed any time to exercise. So, what do they truly value? How can you trust what they say?

Remember, values aren't right or wrong – they motivate you and set your priorities. If you're not motivated to do something or spend time on something, it probably means it isn't connected to one of your values and that's OK. There's no point pretending to value something when clearly, you don't. It leads to mistrust. The point is you need to be honest with yourself. Be clear about your values and your legacy and keep them front of mind when deciding what to do with your time so your actions are congruent and authentic.

TIPS FOR OWNING YOUR TIME

- Gain clarity on your values, beliefs, goals and legacy (see Chapter 3).

- Plan your time daily, weekly, monthly and yearly, with your priorities at the top of the list. Be accountable to a mentor or colleague. Communicate your priorities so everyone knows them.

- Break down your goals into achievable tasks. You'll feel a sense of achievement and see that you're moving forward.

- Create space for yourself before agreeing or disagreeing to something. Don't respond automatically. If your standard response is no, you may miss an opportunity. If your standard response is yes, you may rob yourself of time for your priorities. So, stop. Create space. Reflect and think before committing to something and making a promise.

Busyness makes us stop caring about the things we care about.

MARK BUCHANAN

CHAPTER 4.6

Tell
your story

Share your truth and wisdom

*"We have stories to tell, stories that provide wisdom about the
journey of life. What more have we to give one another than our
"truth" about human adventure as honestly and as openly as we
know how?"*

– RABBI SAUL RUBIN

Storytelling is one of the most powerful skills you can have as an
authentic leader. People have been telling stories since the dawn
of time. Strong cultures throughout history have shared their
beliefs and values through stories, some of which have become
legends that are passed from generation to generation by their
leaders. If you want to have influence, make storytelling part of
your leadership toolkit.

CHAPTER 4.6

For example, as a young lawyer, I was told about the importance of client care. I was informed of the steps I needed to take to build a rapport with the client, how to address the client and how to conduct an interview, and I thought, "Blah, blah, blah ... yeah, yeah. I've got it. Client care. It's important."

Then one of the partners shared with me a story. He said that one stinking hot day, he had to see a new client and his wife on their property west of Toowoomba. When he arrived, it was hard not to notice the mess inside the house. Dishes were piled in the sink and the kitchen benches were untidy. He sat down at the kitchen table to talk to the client when he noticed a cake in the middle of the table, baked by the wife especially for him. The icing was melting off the cake and it was covered in flies. I asked the partner, "So what did you do? Did you eat the cake?" The partner looked me in the eye and said, "Of course I ate the cake. You always eat the f** cake."

Bingo. Lesson learnt. That story was told to me more than 15 years ago and I still remember it. I remembered it every time I dealt with a client during my legal career, the words "eat the f** cake" ringing in my head.

After hearing that story, there was no doubt in my mind what was expected of me and what was meant by client care and rapport. No manual, training session or 10-step instruction guide could have told me more than that one simple yet powerful story.
When you give people instructions and information in a standard way – e.g. by telling them what is right or wrong and what you want them to do – it's often filed away, never to be retrieved again. They may have some fleeting interest in what you're saying but there is no change in their knowledge or behaviours. They have no meaningful connection with what you're saying.

However, people react to stories and narrative in an entirely different way. We process stories through immersion – by putting ourselves in the story. We ask ourselves what we would do in the situation, calling on our own ideas and experience and making the story something we can relate to. That's why storytelling creates changes of opinion and knowledge that *lasts*.

As a leader, you can tell stories to illustrate desired behaviours, explain your values, share a lesson, clarify your strategic goals or describe a vision. Storytelling has so many benefits. Firstly, stories build trust. Your stories reveal who you are and your personality. They connect you with your people, transmitting information and your personal experience. Secondly, they can be used to convey concepts or ideas that might otherwise be difficult to articulate, such as a complicated process.

Most importantly, stories inspire others to act. Leaders are often concerned about *what* they want to tell people or *how* they want to tell people something. But your first question should be, "How do I want to make them *feel*?" Stories that evoke imagination and emotion can be highly persuasive. We remember what we feel.

And, let's face it, stories are fun. Would you rather tell someone what to do or show them through a story? Telling people is not motivating. But a story that makes people join the dots and experience that real "a-ha" moment is powerful. By allowing your people to unpack the story for themselves, you make a lasting impact. You pull people in rather than push your message, and you invite them to come along for the journey and participate.

TIPS FOR EFFECTIVE STORYTELLING

- Always check your intention for telling a story. Do you want to reveal a genuine part of yourself, build trust, connect people, share a lesson learnt or impart knowledge? (All great reasons). Or do you want to manipulate others or make yourself look good? If that's the case, you might end up doing the opposite.

- Bring your story to life by evoking all the senses. What did you see, hear, feel, smell, and taste? Immerse your people in the experience and paint a picture. Take them on a journey. In *The Hero with a Thousand Faces*, author Joseph Campbell describes the idea of a monomyth, an archetypal narrative structure that describes the hero's journey. The hero's journey starts with an ordinary person who experiences a call to adventure. Then there is a three-part structure comprised of the departure or challenge, the action and transformation, and finally the return. This structure gives stories a simple yet powerful framework. Each story needs conflict and resolution, tension and release, mystery and revelation. There must be losses and triumphs, peaks and troughs.

- Take time to craft your stories and practice them. Make them compelling. I always giggle when people hear a speaker and say what a wonderful, natural storyteller they are. Of course, they might be, but chances are they have spent a lot of time and energy crafting and practising the right delivery. They have received feedback on their stories and reworked them.

- Ensure there is simplicity in your story. Choose your words carefully. No one wants a long-winded version. There is an art to including just enough detail to set the scene and evoke emotion without cluttering your story and losing your audience. Every sentence must add to the story.

- Take care to select the right story to tell at the right time and to the right audience. Stories about failing and learning from your mistakes pull people in. Stories that serve only to self-promote turn people away.

- Tell the truth, the whole truth. If you leave the bad bits out of the story, you build distrust. You need to be vulnerable with your storytelling and have the courage to tell your truth. It's the pain people will learn from the most.

- People want to feel you have experienced their problems, pain and fear. They also want to know how you overcame them. Stories that feel familiar – "I've been there, too" – are the most powerful because they're relatable. The audience can imagine themselves in the story, being the hero of their own journey, and are more likely to connect with and remember what you're saying.

*Stories make us more alive,
more human, more courageous,
more loving.*

MADELEINE L'ENGLE

CHAPTER 4.7

Put yourself first

Practise self-care

I often think back to a conversation I had with my Mum when my first son, Tom, was only a small baby. I was sitting in the lounge room and there was a lot of crying, except it wasn't the baby, it was me. Tom wasn't well and I was feeling run down, tired and frustrated. Why couldn't I feed this baby? I felt completely inadequate as a mother. It was like I had lost myself and my place in the world. I felt like I was never going to be good at this parenting gig.

I remember my beautiful, wise Mum looking me in the eye and saying it was time to put myself first. She said, "You'll be no use to this baby or anyone else if you don't take the time to take care of yourself first. You are number one."

At that time, it felt strange and unnatural to put me before my baby. I mean, he was a baby, right? I had to tend to his needs first. There was no time for myself, or so I thought.

I now find myself having similar conversations with leaders. As a leader, you can become so focussed on the huge responsibility of looking after your team members that you forget to look after yourself. You are so concerned about your team's development, learning opportunities and goals that your own personal and professional development needs get put on the back burner. Yes, your team members need you and they rely on you, but to lead them effectively, you need to be at your best.

Let me ask you this: as a leader, has it ever come to the end of the day, say 5-5.30pm, and you've realised you haven't done anything on your own to-do list? You've spent your entire day putting out fires, being interrupted and dealing with urgent emails. It's not until the end of the day that you get to start your own work. If you're always putting in long hours, sending emails at midnight and on weekends, you need to ask yourself: "How long can this continue?" When you put your family, partner, team members and everything else before yourself, are you truly giving 100%?

You need to come first. As my Mum said, you are number one. Don't make the mistake of getting so caught up giving your time and energy to others that you forget to give time to yourself. As author Paulo Coelho says, "When you say 'yes' to others, make sure you are not saying 'no' to yourself." An important step to building your confidence is to care for you, your body and your mind. It's vital to have time to yourself.

Think of the instructions given during the pre-flight announcement on a plane. The flight attendant tells you that if there is a change in cabin pressure during the flight, you must put your own oxygen mask on *before* helping others. This is a great metaphor for caring for ourselves, and it seems obvious, right? Then why is it so difficult for us to do in our everyday lives? Is it socially acceptable, or even applauded, for a woman to be selfless and put the needs of others first? Is this where our self-worth comes from? Are we comfortable with this self-sacrifice? Is it a badge of honour we wear as women?

When you put yourself first or say no to others, do you feel guilty? Do you feel selfish? Maybe part of you feels this way, particularly when others depend on you – an elderly parent, young children or junior team members. But that's the point. If you have people depending on you, what happens if something happens to *you*?

If you don't put your own oxygen mask on first, you'll be on the floor unconscious, unable to help anyone. In fact, you'll be the person people will have to save – and that's if you're lucky because they might step over you to get to the exit.

When you constantly feel fatigued, anxious and burnt out, it affects your relationships and can even cause relationship breakdowns. You may reach a breaking point when the issue escalates to one of absolute self-preservation. It is no longer about the small, everyday contributions you can make to yourself – it becomes much bigger and much more serious. It's a time when your self-confidence is at an all-time low. You're on the treadmill of life and you run, run, run, feeling that you have no time to look after yourself until your body or mind screams at you to stop, take a break and get off the treadmill.

In Dr Adam Fraser's book *The Third Space*, he discusses a mentoring session with a senior female leader. When describing her life, she said she felt like a hamster on a wheel, going round and round, except the hamster was dead and the wheel kept spinning. Yikes!

I've mentored many women who have reached a point in their corporate careers when they have felt they have nothing left to give. Everything seems too hard and there is too much pressure. Unfortunately, sometimes it takes getting to this point to realise you need to make significant changes in your life (see the "Reboot your life" section in Chapter 3).

At the start of each day, ask yourself, "What am I going to do for myself today?" Make a promise to yourself and be accountable. Think about the things, the people, the activities and the work that gives you energy, joy and fulfilment. It is your job to make these things your number-one priority.

If you've spent a long time (maybe even a lifetime) putting everyone else before yourself, changing this habit can be tough. It may take some time. It will involve thinking differently about yourself, what you have to offer and how you can be the best version of you. It will also mean acknowledging and addressing your own feelings. It may require some long overdue discussions with your partner, children, boss or team members about what you need to do not only to be at your best but to be there for them in the long term.

If you put yourself first and practise self-care, you'll be able to show up more fully and have more presence in your personal and professional relationships. You will have more energy, more patience and less anxiety. In fact, seven out of 10 women report feeling more confident or positive when they invest time in caring for themselves.[1]

---

1 Moss, R. "Women's Body Confidence Is A 'Critical Issue' Worldwide, Warns Dove's Largest Ever Report." *Huffington Post*, 21 June, 2016. http://www.huffingtonpost.co.uk/entry/dove-global-body-image-report_uk_5762a6a1e4b0681487dcc470

As a leader, you will be more productive in the office and more focussed on the tasks that matter. A happy leader makes a happy team.

So, practise self-care every day. Don't wait until you get to burn-out point or self-preservation mode. Put on your oxygen mask now and breathe.

WAYS TO PRACTISE SELF-CARE

- **At work.** Take a walk during your lunch hour; attend a webcast; listen to a podcast; share your feelings with a trusted colleague; attend an event with like-minded professionals; invest in a mentor; book your next annual leave.

  Whatever you do, it's important you allocate time in your day for "me time". You need a chance to rewind and recharge. Avoid interruptions and distractions. If you use that time to drink a coffee, don't read your emails at the same time – switch off, savour the taste and relax.

- **At home.** Read an inspiring book or your favourite magazine; listen to music that makes you happy; dance; buy yourself a bunch of fresh flowers; write in your journal; call a friend who makes you laugh; take a fun class – something you've always wanted to learn; get out in nature.

  Keep your time at home separate from your work so you can truly unwind.

You, yourself, as much as anyone else in the entire universe, deserve your love and attention.

BUDDHA

CHAPTER 4.8

Stop reacting

Create space to be yourself

I have a confession to make. I have a hiding spot in my house. And I don't mean a hiding place for when I play hide and seek with the kids – I mean a place to physically get away from everyone and everything.

You see, there are times as a mother when I feel I'm going to lose it, completely blow up. Things build up to a point with my three kids that I feel like I'm about to explode. I know if I don't run, I'll be the kind of mother I don't want to be. Hence, the hiding place.

My hiding spot, which I've nicknamed my "retreat", is inside my walk-in wardrobe, where I sit cross-legged on the floor between my handbags and shoes. I just sit and breathe. I slow down. I listen to my breath and block everything else out.

CHAPTER 4.8

There are times when I can hear the kids calling to me. "Mum! Mum! Where are you, Mum?" I ignore them. Then I hear the little buggers working together. It seems that whatever they were fighting over is long forgotten, and I hear them saying to each other, "Where is she? Where could she be? Where do you think Mum's gone?"

Once I've calmed down, I head back downstairs and magically reappear beside my kids. At that point, I'm ready to sort things out peacefully, or if it wasn't a big deal to carry on with the day. It's all about picking your battles, right?

As a mother, I know being reactive is something I need to watch. I know when I give in to that reactive side of my personality, it never ends well. It was the same in the office. I can be emotional. I wear my heart on my sleeve. I'm easy to read and I'm very honest. It's my strength and my flaw.

The problem with reactive behaviour is that it gets in the way of you being able to be the real you. When you react, it's all about what's happening in that moment. High emotion is often involved and you are in fight or flight mode – the physiological reaction humans experience when we feel under threat. When your body receives a message from the brain that you're in a stressful situation, it releases adrenaline, norepinephrine and cortisol. These hormones give you a surge of energy – your heart pounds, your muscles tense, your breathing quickens and you sweat.[1] You're ready to flee or fight the real or perceived threat.

When you're in this state and react automatically, you say and do things that are not aligned with your values, beliefs or legacy. You give in to all that emotion. This can feel great at the time. You get it

---

1 Klein, S. "Adrenaline, Cortisol, Norepinephrine: The Three Major Stress Hormones, Explained." *Huffington Post*, 19 April, 2013. http://www.huffingtonpost.com.au/entry/adrenaline-cortisol-stress-hormones_n_3112800

all out and it's a quick release. However, later when you think about your behaviour and what you said and how you reacted, you beat yourself up.

Have you ever had a conversation during the day, then later at night replayed the conversation word-by-word, thinking about what else you could have said or how else you could have responded, and you felt sick about it?

I remember having a conversation at work with two fellow partners about a course we were going to run for an external group of participants. The learning team, which I was part of, had come up with a proposal and curriculum based on what we believed were the requirements. In the meeting, I presented our thoughts to the partners and it was clear it wasn't what they had in mind. I don't know why, maybe I was under pressure at home or maybe I had other things on my mind, but I lost it in that meeting. Big time. I overreacted because of my emotional state and it made a huge impact on my relationship with my fellow partners and how I felt about myself. I was full of regret and remorse and, of course, I had to patch up the relationship with those people afterwards.

As a leader, eyes are on you all the time. Everything you say and do is being watched. Your reputation and brand are built with every conversation and interaction, so consistency is important. Sometimes you need some space to think so you can respond to situations effectively and authentically.

So, how can you create this space when emotions are high? A simple yet effective way is to take a deep breath or two and count to 10. Then, go for a walk and reflect on the leader you want to be. Perhaps, like me, you might need to find your own hiding spot. I've even invented meetings to get out of a tricky reactive situation.

"Sorry, I've got to go. I've got a 2 o'clock meeting." I knew I had to get myself out of that room before I said something I would regret.

Sometimes people will try to drag you back when you create this space. They'll want to have the confrontation right there and then. I've had people in my life who have been peeved about me walking away from a conversation or situation. However, in my own mind, I'd rather them be slightly unhappy with me for walking away than destroying our relationship by saying or doing something I didn't mean. In time, they'll forgive the walking away but there are some things once said you can't take back.

Creating that space doesn't mean you hide from a problem or bottle it up. It's about you taking the time you need to thoroughly consider your response.

I received an email one lunchtime when I was facilitating a workshop. It contained some feedback about a webinar. It really got under my skin. I was angry, and I totally disagreed with the feedback. I was just about to send a reply and CC another 10 people into my email when my good friend Debbie came in and said, "Midja, you're on. It's time to start the session again." I had to leave the email. At 5 o'clock that afternoon when I had finished presenting and was in a great mood, I walked back to my room and read the email again. I sent a one-sentence response back. It said, "Thank you very much for your feedback."

You see, when you create space, you realise what matters most. You get back in touch with your values, who you are, what you're about and the legacy you want to leave. You respond very differently to how you would have in the heat of the moment.

To be your true, authentic self, sometimes you need to give yourself a time out. **Remember, you are always responsible for how you act, no matter how you feel.**

QUESTIONS FOR YOU TO CONSIDER

1. When do you find yourself responding reactively? Is there a particular person, activity or situation that triggers your reaction?

   _____

   _____

   _____

   _____

   _____

2. What do you say, do, think and feel in the heat of the moment?

   _____

   _____

   _____

   _____

3. What impact does this have on you, your relationships and your work?

   _____

   _____

   _____

   _____

4. Is your reactive response consistent with your values, beliefs and legacy?

_____

_____

_____

_____

_____

5. What could you do to create space when you are next faced with this trigger?

_____

_____

_____

_____

_____

6. What would this look and feel like? What would be the outcome?

_____

_____

_____

_____

_____

Between stimulus and response there is a space. In that space is our power to choose our response. In our response lies our growth and our freedom.

VIKTOR FRANKL

CHAPTER 4.9

Take off your armour

Be vulnerable

On International Women's Day, a quote kept popping up in my social media feed. It was this: "Here's to strong women. May we know them. May we be them. May we raise them."

This quote got me thinking about what we mean by the word "strength". Traditionally, we think that to be strong, we need to fight. We need to be tough, competitive, goal-oriented, rational and linear. These terms are often associated with strong leadership and commonly considered more masculine in nature.

However, can't strength be the opposite? Instead of fighting, instead of putting up walls, isn't it strong to let the walls down and have the courage to be vulnerable? Can't strength be associated with the "feminine" traits of intuition, collaboration, emotion, passion and empathy? Research professor Brené Brown, in her book *Daring Greatly*, says: "Vulnerability is not weakness, and the uncertainty, risk, and emotional exposure we face every day are not optional. Our only choice is a question of engagement. Our willingness to own and engage with our vulnerability determines the depth of our courage and the clarity of our purpose. The level to which we protect ourselves from being vulnerable is a measure of our fear and disconnection."

To show yourself to the world, to be authentic and genuine, you must be vulnerable. The courage to be vulnerable comes from truly knowing yourself, your values, your beliefs, your purpose and your legacy. When you don't do this, it's like wearing a coat of armour. When you're unsure of yourself, when your self-worth and self-esteem come from the need to be right (that traditional view of strength), you need to put your armour on for protection. You put it on because you don't want to be hurt. You don't want people to judge you or see the real you. Your armour serves a purpose, and without it, you feel exposed and fear you'll get taken advantage of.

I agree that without the armour, you might get hurt and you might feel pain, but you also get to feel love and joy and connection. The only time you'll feel hurt is when you've built your confidence on what other people think of you instead of what you think of yourself. If you are confident, if you have an unwavering self-belief, you can take the armour off and know you'll be OK.

As a female leader, it can often feel as though you're going into battle. You feel you must fight for your voice to be heard, fight for resources, fight for recognition and fight for your team members. You head into meetings wearing your coat of armour because it gives you strength. It makes you feel invincible. Now, imagine that everyone else at the leadership table is wearing their coat of armour, too. How does it feel? When everyone wears their armour, there is no opportunity to connect. You bump against one another in a competitive way. It slows everyone down. It stops you from being agile. You can't see the real person under the armour and everyone looks the same.

It's time to take the armour off. You don't need it. Your power comes from your authenticity, by knowing yourself and being yourself. You've got this. When you take the armour off, you'll feel lighter. You'll feel more like you. People will be able to see the real you and connect with you as a leader.

The great thing is that once you take your armour off and become vulnerable, other people will feel safe to do the same. What a different leadership table you'll be sitting at! When everyone takes off their armour, you can connect with one another, see one another, really listen to and understand one another. You might have different points of view, but you will use this diversity to create synergy and innovation, not competition.

Now, I'm not saying that you let everything hang out all the time! Vulnerability doesn't mean you should share *everything* with *everyone*. It's about being true to yourself. Sometimes you may not want to share or feel the need to share. There might not be enough trust in the relationship yet or it might not be the right situation to share openly. And that's OK. You can still acknowledge your feelings and beliefs to yourself even if you don't outwardly share them.

THE SPECTRUM OF SHARING

UNDERSHARING   **AUTHENTICITY**   **OVERSHARING**

- **Undersharing:** This is when the armour is on. It's a bit like wanting to tap on someone's chest and ask, "Hello, who's in there?" At this end of the spectrum, people feel they don't know the real you. Because you reveal so little, people suspect a hidden agenda and there is scepticism about your ability to lead. People will be unable to make an emotional commitment to you as a leader because they don't know who you really are. There is disconnection and distrust.

- **Oversharing:** At the other end of the spectrum, when you share too much too early, it makes others feel uncomfortable. Oversharing and sharing for all the wrong reasons create doubt about your leadership motives and makes you appear self-absorbed and ego-driven. "It's all about me." The end result is the same: disconnection and distrust.

- **Authenticity:** Then comes the sweet spot in the middle. This is where you can be open, honest and vulnerable in an appropriate way. This is where you build high trust with others and make a real connection.

You will never feel so strong as you do once you take off your armour. Don't ever hide your magnificent self. You can be vulnerable and you can be real. **You don't need a coat of armour to keep you protected, you have something better: your CONFIDENCE.**

QUESTIONS TO HELP YOU TAKE OFF YOUR ARMOUR

Every interaction you have, every conversation you engage in, is a chance to show yourself and build a real connection. It's about assessing each situation and asking yourself:

- Do I feel safe to show my true self?

- What's my intention in sharing my opinion, belief, feelings or story? Am I sharing to build trust, connect with and serve others? Or am I sharing to prove I'm right and feed my ego?

- What's the current level of trust in this relationship?

- Is this the appropriate time and situation to share?

- What are the possible benefits and risks in taking off my armour?

In order for connection to happen, we have to allow ourselves to be seen, really seen.

BRENÉ BROWN

CHAPTER 4.10

Create your brand

Set yourself apart from others

When you create a strong brand, you show yourself to the world. Everything you have explored in this chapter contributes to the creation of your brand. It tells your story and sets you apart from others.

Your brand is the way other people see you. It's what you're known for and what you represent. As Jeff Bezos, founder and CEO of Amazon, says: "Your brand is what others say about you when you're not in the room." It's comprised of your ideas, your values, your expertise and your style. To be memorable, it needs to be distinctive, visible and consistent.

When you create a strong leadership brand, it gives you influence. It opens opportunities for you and the people you lead, allowing you to make a bigger difference and scale up your expertise and ideas.

This is more important now than ever. Why? Because by 2020, more than 50% of the US workforce will be self-employed.[1] It's safe to say Australia will see a similar trend. This means that as a leader, you need to be able to set yourself apart from the competition. In other words, to lead with influence, you need to sell yourself. To cut through the noise, you need to market your skills and talents through a strong brand.

Be your brand's designer. Don't let it develop by default. If you don't act now to brand yourself, others will on your behalf. You'll be judged purely by what others say about you. It's up to you to show the world who you are through what you say and what you do.

Your brand is a personal promise to your people. It tells them what they can expect from you. In a leadership role, you need to keep this promise and exceed expectations to build trust and commitment.

The most important thing to remember about your brand is that it must always be based on your authentic self. Start with your values, beliefs, purpose, magic and legacy. All the elements we explored in the Know Yourself chapter are needed to create a brand that is congruent with your character and who you are at roots level.

If you try to build a brand without doing the work on yourself first and without a deep level of self-awareness, you can destroy the trust other people have in you. People can detect when your brand is fake. You may be able to pretend to be someone you're not

1 Rashid, B. "The Rise Of The Freelancer Economy." *Forbes*, 26 January, 2016. https://www.forbes.com/sites/brianrashid/2016/01/26/the-rise-of-the-freelancer-econo-my/#4496dbdd3bdf

for a short while, but you won't be able to sustain it. It's too hard. Your behaviour will be inconsistent and unpredictable, and you'll struggle to live up to the brand you try to portray, letting people down.

As a female leader, don't lose your beautiful feminine qualities when you climb the corporate ladder. Don't believe that you have to become like the other leaders already sitting at the table. Your unique skills, behaviours and way of thinking are exactly what is needed.

Be steadfast. Know what you stand for. Act according to your purpose, strengths and expertise. At some point in your career, people will get to know the real you. This usually happens when you are faced with a challenging time. It's easy to maintain appearances when the sun is shining, but once the storm hits, your character – the roots of your confidence tree – is exposed. At this point, if your character doesn't match your brand and who you say you are, you will lose the trust of your people and lose your influence as a leader.

Of course, your brand will evolve over time. It needs to, because your values and priorities will change. Your personal brand will become stronger and more distinctive as you gain greater insight into your purpose and who you are as a leader.

Think about what you can do every day to build your personal brand so it is congruent with who you really are.

HOW TO CREATE YOUR BRAND

- Tell your story. Authentic storytelling is a huge part of building your brand (see "Tell your story" in this chapter).

- Consider what you say yes to and what you say no to. Where you spend your time says a lot about what you value (see "Own your time" in this chapter).

- Your outward appearance impacts your brand. Be deliberate about how you dress, how you look, how you walk and how you talk.

- Ensure your online personality is consistent with your brand and who you are. Be consistent with your message on social media and be cautious about what you "like".

- Let your personality shine through. People want to know the real you. They want to know what's underneath the suit (see "Take off your armour" in this chapter). What are your interests outside of work? I've known leaders who love surfing, who are coffee fanatics, who are foodies, who adore their miniature schnauzers or who cycle every day to work. Share these passions with your people.

- Be visible. Leadership is like a contact sport. It doesn't happen behind a desk. You must get out there and meet people.

- Make every interaction count. Everything you say or do will add to your brand.

*In order to be irreplaceable,
one must always be different.*

COCO CHANEL

CHAPTER 5

BELIEVE IN YOURSELF

CHAPTER 5

Believe
in yourself

You now *know* yourself and can *be* yourself. Now, it's time to *believe* in yourself.

You have the tools to be your true authentic self but what you don't realise is that your authentic self is *extraordinary*. You still don't have that strong, unwavering self-belief. The kind of belief that makes you unshakeable. Your confidence tree is growing but you've not yet reached the top. You are not yet unshakeable.

You still hear that negative voice in your head, judging you and comparing you with others. You place too much weight on what others think of you and their expectations. Without a strong belief in yourself, the predefined perceptions and limitations you've placed on yourself can make you want to give up. You feel held back and you underestimate yourself.

Evidence shows that men tend to overestimate their abilities and performance while women underestimate theirs. This is despite there being no difference in the quality of their performance.[1] Furthermore, internal statistics from Hewlett-Packard found that women only apply for a promotion when they believe they meet 100% of the qualifications for the job. Men, however, are happy to apply if they think they can meet 60% of the job requirements.[2] So, we have all these amazing overqualified women who doubt themselves and, therefore, hold themselves back. Men doubt themselves as well sometimes, but they don't let their doubts stop them as often as women do.

So many women don't realise their full potential. Why? They don't believe in themselves strongly enough. At the first hurdle, they give up. But if you firmly believe in yourself, you'll back yourself. You'll see failure and mistakes as par for the course. If you're not failing, you're not learning. After all, failure is only a temporary state.

You started life with no preconceived ideas of what you could or couldn't do. For a young child, the question, "What do you want to be when you grow up?", holds infinite possibilities. Do you remember what that felt like?

However, over time, life has taught you to limit yourself, to shrink your dreams and dial down your imagination and enthusiasm. It's time to dial them back up.

It's time to change your thinking and believe in yourself. People are already looking at you for inspiration and leadership. They sense your authenticity and, as a result, they trust you. As you start to believe in yourself, your people will believe in you as well.

---

1 Kay, K. and Shipman, C. "The Confidence Gap." *The Atlantic*, May 2014. https://www.theatlantic.com/magazine/archive/2014/05/the-confidence-gap/359815/

2 Clark, N. "Act Now To Shrink The Confidence Gap." *Forbes*, 28 April, 2014. https://www.forbes.com/sites/womensmedia/2014/04/28/act-now-to-shrink-the-confidence-gap/#6e56f3b15c41

In this chapter, you will learn how to:

- Stop the comparisons
- Risk more rejection
- Find your tribe
- Practise gratitude
- Keep life light
- Stop the judgement
- Take action and repeat
- Let go of others' expectations
- Change your self-talk
- Take the compliment

*You don't become what you want,
you become what you believe.*

OPRAH WINFREY

CHAPTER 5.1

Stop the comparisons

Focus on you

Do you ever compare yourself to others? How well do you stack up? Do you allow these comparisons to determine your self-worth?

I've been guilty of comparing my life to the lives of my friends, family and colleagues – comparing my success, career, intelligence, relationships and wealth. As a young lawyer, I remember looking at the other lawyers in the firm and comparing myself. *She's billed more than me this month. He's so much better at negotiating than I am. Clients seem to really connect with her.* What a waste of energy! Comparing yourself is time spent focussing on others when you could be focussing on yourself. Comparisons are unnecessary, unhelpful and rarely accurate.

If you compare yourself to others and base your self-worth and confidence on these comparisons, you do yourself an injustice. You are unique with your own strengths, talent and opportunities.

There was a time when people looking at my life from the outside would have thought it was perfect. I was married with three kids, living on the Gold Coast, a partner in a law firm. People thought my life was flawless. But looks can be deceiving. When I told people my marriage was over and things had not been good for a long time, they were shocked.

You see, people only show you a small piece of their life, then you take that small piece and interpret it and compare it to your life. It's so easy to do. Of course, now it's easier than ever with social media. Now we can see what our "friends" (and I use that term loosely) are doing every part of the day and night.

Social media posts do not equal real life. A post is just a happy snapshot. It's a tiny part of someone's life that they have selected and filtered. I know I've often posted a smiling, loving family photo at dinner only to be screaming at the kids 10 minutes later. I'm not posting, "Here I am on a Tuesday night doing my third load of washing #whoseideawasthreechildren," or, "Here I am on a Saturday night home by myself again #midjacantgetadate."

You see, Facebook and Instagram posts are people's highlight reel. They are the moments people are proud of and they want to share. It's the perception they want you to have of their life.

So, it's important for your own self-belief that you put all this into context and see it for what it really is. If you spend your time and energy looking at other people's posts and feeling sorry for yourself, feeling less because of how you perceive your own life – what a waste of time!

A couple of years ago, the kids and I headed up to Poona (north of the Sunshine Coast in Queensland) for a long weekend with friends. It was our annual Christmas get-together. As we got closer to our destination, I noticed the service bars on my mobile had dipped to two, then one. By the time we arrived at our destination, I jumped out of the car, grabbed my phone and to my despair read the words that elicit fear in any social media-savvy person: SOS only. AGHHHHHH!

I was facing three days without Facebook, Instagram, Snapchat and texts — what was I going to do? Now, I must admit, I felt slightly anxious and nauseous. At one point, I could be seen down the street, sitting in the gutter with my phone at arm's length reaching towards the heavens, trying to get some type of service — even one bar.

You see, I'm a big fan of social media and its benefits. However, I understand that sometimes it can have a negative impact on our lives. One of these downsides can be when we use it to compare our lives to others to see how we stack up and measure our self-worth.

You need to be able to identify when someone is motivating and inspiring you and when they are having a negative impact on your self-esteem. If sharing in someone's life brings out the best in you and makes you strive to achieve your own goals, keep them in your life. But if someone makes you feel less and not good enough, then you need to remove them from your life. Otherwise, they will continue to drain your energy. If they are on social media, stop following them. Unfriend them. It's like anything in your life, if it's not bringing you something positive, stop it. Do a clean-out.

Stop idolising people and start humanising them. There is always more than meets the eye to every situation. Everyone is unique and we all go through different stages in our lives and careers: the ups and downs, the swings and the roundabouts. Once you realise this, then you can truly enjoy and celebrate your special moments and the special moments of your friends. You will stop comparing and be genuinely happy for others and their achievements, knowing you have your own unique strengths. Even if things may not be going so well for you, your time will come. As one of my friends says, "Tide comes in and tide goes out."

And you know what? The three days in Poona being disconnected and not knowing what anyone else was doing was kind of nice. I was able to focus on myself and the people around me – no comparisons, just a chance to be happy with me.

QUESTIONS FOR YOU TO CONSIDER

1. How often do you compare yourself to others? In what ways?

   _____

   _____

   _____

   _____

   _____

2. Do you experience feelings of self-doubt and inadequacy from these comparisons?

   _____

   _____

   _____

   _____

   _____

3. Do you feel upbeat and positive or envious and negative after scrolling through your social media feed?

   _____

   _____

   _____

   _____

   _____

4. How do you genuinely feel when someone close to you succeeds at something you want to succeed at?

_____

_____

_____

_____

_____

5. Do you feel in competition with those you work with or do you feel a sense of collaboration?

_____

_____

_____

_____

_____

Comparison is the thief of joy.

THEODORE ROOSEVELT

CHAPTER 5.2

Risk more rejection

You're not for everyone

In the first year after leaving my role in the law firm, I started applying for work. I remember feeling the sting of rejection. One Friday afternoon, I received a "thanks but no thanks" email from an organisation I had applied to do some lecturing for. I thought I'd be able to make a real contribution to the organisation and students, but they obviously didn't feel the same way.

I felt a little sorry for myself. Rejection can do that to you. That night, I was meant to attend going away drinks for a colleague. I was excited to catch up with friends but I was still feeling the sting of that rejection email. However, I'm not one to turn down a night out (as those of you who know me well can vouch for), so off I went, determined to put the email behind me and have a good time.

CHAPTER 5.2

I'd been at the gathering at a bar in Broadbeach for half an hour when I received another blow. A guy I had dated walked in. He, too, had given me the big "thanks but no thanks" and it was the first time I'd seen him since he ghosted me. (For those not familiar with the concept, ghosting is the term used to describe when you're dating someone and they stop texting you or disappear). Now, like the job I'd applied for, I thought we would be a great match. I'd thought we could contribute to each other's lives and that we really suited one another, but like the organisation, he didn't feel the same way. That Friday was painful and, ouch, I felt the sting of rejection.

It can hurt when someone doesn't want you personally or professionally. It always amuses me when people say, "Just don't take it personally." I mean, how else are you supposed to take it? Maybe they mean don't let it impact the way you feel about yourself. I agree with that. Just because someone or some organisation doesn't see your worth, it doesn't mean you're worth any less. It means that everything you are, your values, your strengths, your beliefs, your skills, your behaviours, are not for them. It's not what they're looking for now or maybe ever.

When you're hit with rejection, you need to be strong and hold steady. This can be tough, particularly when you feel like it's coming at you from a number of directions.

You need to remember that you can't be everything to everyone. Not everyone is going to connect with you. If you never experience rejection, chances are you're not being authentic and true to yourself. You're placing a high priority on being liked. You're changing your viewpoints and behaviour to suit those around you. You're like the tree with shallow roots, swaying in the breeze, agreeing with everyone and wanting to be liked, wanting to be accepted. If you lack confidence, you see rejection as a huge risk and you fear it. You try to avoid it at all costs and it keeps you squarely in your comfort zone.

But when you are confident, you view rejection differently. It's a risk you're willing to take. Rejection means you're being yourself. You're authentic, you're real and you're steadfast in who you are and what you believe in. You have developed your strengths and accepted your weaknesses and you are either what someone wants or you're not. It's as simple as that. The faster someone is either for you or against you, the stronger and more definite you are. Not everyone wants or needs your magic, and that's perfect because you haven't got the time or energy to give it to everyone. You want to have personal and professional relationships with people who connect with you and who know you will make a difference in their lives.

If you let go of the fear of rejection and accept it as a risk, you can share your ideas willingly and open yourself up to new possibilities. I know that my practice, this book, my programs and my corporate work are not for everyone. They're not for every woman and they're not for every organisation, and that's OK. There will be people who want to be part of your team, who want to follow you as a leader, and then there will be other people who don't have that connection with you.

I love using the phrase, "So what?" I think it brings context to a situation. So what if you got rejected from that position? So what if you don't get a second phone call back from that guy you went on a date with? So what? You are who you are, and you are true to yourself and that's all you can do. You can be confident and you can let go of the fear of rejection.

CHAPTER 5.2

If you let rejection impact how you see yourself, it takes away your power. Sometimes, you won't even know why someone rejected you, and you will make up excuses. You'll make all sorts of assumptions, which is unfair to yourself. It can also impact your relationships. But if you are OK with rejection, you can move on. You don't hold grudges. You don't go for revenge. It doesn't get nasty. You might even be able to work again with that person or organisation in the future. I've had professional relationships where I wasn't wanted or needed at a certain time, then a year or two later, I've worked with that organisation because it's been the right time and the right place to do the work I'm meant to do.

In fact, you may not see it at the time, but sometimes rejection turns out to be just what you needed. I stumbled across this quote, which I often remind myself of: "Sometimes, the universe takes away what you think you want to make room for what you deserve." The role I applied for and didn't get – not meant to be. That guy who didn't want to see me again – not meant to be.

How you deal with rejection and hardship shows your true character. It shows confidence. And I know it's annoying to hear, but I think rejection can be character building. If your confidence tree has strong roots, if you know yourself and you show yourself in the face of rejection, in the face of thanks but no thanks, you stand tall. Don't let anyone take your confidence and power away.

TIPS TO HANDLE REJECTION

- Accept the rejection and don't play the blame game.

- Talk it out with a trusted friend (wine optional!).

- Get feedback if possible. It's all valuable information.

- Reflect on what you could have done differently and what you've learnt from the experience.

- Take time out if you need to. You're allowed to be upset.

- Remind yourself how amazing you are. Remember your magic.

- Put the rejection into context. Ask the question, "So what?"

- Do something for yourself – something fun.

- Finally, let it go and move forward.

Confidence is not, "They will like me." Confidence instead is, "I'll be fine if they don't."

CHRISTINA GRIMMIE

CHAPTER 5.3

Find your tribe

The rush of belonging

When I think about my tribe, I smile. They make me laugh, they support me, challenge me, inspire me and make me see things differently. They give me energy and lift me up, and I hope I do the same for them. The people closest to me – my tribe, my inner circle – believe in me before I even believe in myself. Some members have been in the tribe a long time; others have come and gone but they have all played an important role in my life.

All of us have a need to belong. We want to fit in and feel understood – it's one of our most fundamental needs as human beings. Your tribe is a collection of people who understand you. They get you. You might share a common experience, such as work, motherhood, marriage or divorce, or you may share an interest, like yoga, travel, painting or champagne (yes, you can build a tribe based on a love of bubbles!). Your tribe impacts how you see yourself and contributes significantly to the quality of your life. Your confidence starts growing by getting to know yourself and being authentic, but you also need to encourage that growth by connecting with others.

Motivational speaker Jim Rohn famously said you are the average of the five people you spend the most time with. You are your own person and your confidence starts with you, but those around you will always have a degree of influence. That's why it's so important to choose carefully who you let into your tribe. Have you ever walked away from a conversation with someone and felt lighter? Did you feel like you could conquer the world? These are the people you should let into your inner circle.

If you don't have a strong tribe and you let people in who don't belong, it will impact how you feel about yourself. If the people around you doubt you, are negative and rain on your parade, be careful because it might rub off on you. You will take on the traits of the people you hang around with, which is fantastic if they're amazing, happy, confident people, but not so good if they're people who bring you down.

In your busy life, you need as much energy as you can get. The people around you either give you energy or take it away. When there is so much you want to fit into your life, there is no room to spare, so you need to be careful who you give your time to and what you get in return. For a relationship to be effective, there needs to be something in it for both parties. Both sides need to make a positive contribution.

This is why self-belief is critical. When you lack self-belief, you can let people into your tribe who shouldn't be there. I found myself in this situation a couple of years ago. I was in a relationship with a man who didn't treat me well. Let's just say it was all about him all the time, but I couldn't see it. My friends were concerned, of course, and they asked me a lot of questions, some more forcefully than others. We all have those wonderful friends who tell it like it is – no filter. Love these women!

I was at the bottom of the confidence tree during this time. I basically had no idea who I was as a single woman. I guess that happens when you're 18 years out of the dating game. I had very little self-belief and, therefore, my confidence was at an all-time low. I was at the bottom of the tree, not knowing who I was.

I put up with his behaviour; I made that choice. If any of my friends were being treated the way he treated me, I would have flipped out. I wouldn't have allowed it, but I allowed it to happen to me and I know this was because of my lack of confidence. Am I going to beat myself up about it? No, because sometimes it takes time to work on your self-awareness and your self-belief before you can see that someone is not right in your life.

And it's not just the time you spend in the company of these people that is impacted. Their impact is always felt. Even when they're not physically there with you, they feed your fear and your doubts. It's like they're sitting on your shoulder, whispering in your ear that you aren't enough. Well, you are enough and you don't need them. You deserve to be in the company of amazing, generous people who lift you up.

So, be cautious with who you let into your world. The people in a tribe know each other well and trust is paramount. We're at our most vulnerable when we're with those people. We share two things with them. Firstly, we share our fears. Our deepest fears, not only our problems. Problems can be shared with anyone, the person at the supermarket or in the school car park, but it's those closest to us who we share our fears with, those things deep down inside. We only trust the people in our inner circle with our fears because we know we're not going to be judged.

Secondly, we share our dreams with our tribe. Our "someday I'll ..." The almost unspeakable dreams (that niggle inside) we keep from everyone except those closest to us. I read this beautiful quote in one of the books I have from a friend, and it said:

"She keeps the dreams that her friends forget, the ones that seem too big or too distant: built for someone else, and when the moment is right, she returns them to their owners. Reminds them what they've always known. Step-by-step, the stars are reached. Our friends help us do the climbing." – M.H. Clark, *I Am Her*

My question is, are the people around you helping you do the climbing or are they pulling you down?

It is the same in the workplace. Professionally, your connections and the colleagues closest to you reflect your own reputation and can add or take away from your leadership brand. You want relationships with transparency, openness and high trust. This is when the best work is done, when results are achieved, when you don't have to worry about competition, sabotage, what people are thinking or what people are saying behind your back.

All tribes need a leader and if you're in a leadership position, it's your responsibility to connect your people with a common purpose and passion. You need to understand the problems and fears of your people and what's getting in the way of them doing their best work. As a tribal leader, it's not about you, it's about them. You will inspire your tribe by being present, honest and vulnerable, by sharing your stories and deeply listening to others. At times, you may also need to grow your tribe and look for new members who will share your passion and contribute to your mission.

QUESTIONS ABOUT YOUR TRIBE

1. Who are the five people you spend most of your time with – firstly, in your personal life and secondly, in your professional life?

    _____

    _____

    _____

    _____

2. How would you describe these people?

    _____

    _____

    _____

    _____

3. How do you feel after you spend time with them?

    _____

    _____

    _____

    _____

4. Who in your tribe do you want to continue to spend time with and keep close?

    _____

    _____

    _____

One of the most powerful of our survival mechanisms is to be part of a tribe, to contribute to (and take from) a group of like-minded people. We are drawn to leaders and to their ideas, and we can't resist the rush of belonging and the thrill of the new.

SETH GODIN

CHAPTER 5.4

Practise gratitude

Appreciate the small stuff

Practising gratitude is a wonderful way to gain greater self-belief. It's about appreciating others in your life but it's also about appreciating yourself, what you have, what you've achieved and everything about you – your talents, abilities and strengths.

Your self-belief grows from acknowledging and valuing the contributions you make every day, big and small. It's so important to take stock of the difference you make in others' lives. Sometimes you can be in such a rush to move on to the next project or the next big goal, you don't stop to consider and celebrate what you have achieved.

Gratitude means being genuinely thankful for who you are and what you have in your life, instead of focussing on what you don't have.

CHAPTER 5.4

Practising gratitude will help you stop the unhealthy comparisons and the green-eyed monster of envy. It will allow you to be truly happy for the achievements and success of others. You adopt a mentality of abundance, where there is plenty for everyone and someone else's success doesn't impact or lessen your own. You know you don't have to compete. You can build on your successes and be excited about your future. What a wonderful way to live!

Let's face it, we all have so much to be thankful for, particularly the small, everyday moments we can take for granted. I'm sure you've heard the expression, "Don't sweat the small stuff." I totally agree, but I also think we shouldn't ignore the small stuff. For most of us, on most days, the small stuff is all we have. Now, I have a great life, a fortunate life, but most days I'm at home doing the school run, putting the washing on and writing at the kitchen table. That's about as exciting as life gets. No Beyoncé moments for me, I'm afraid.

Of course, at times we have big events to look forward to. The huge moments and milestones, such as birthday celebrations, work promotions, weddings, births, etc. However, these don't happen every day, so you need to see the magic in the small stuff; those little moments every day when you get to make a difference, be yourself, learn something new, experience nature or share something with a friend – the peaceful moments and the crazy, fun ones.

Some of the small stuff I'm grateful for: the sun on my skin, a perfect cold beer, a swim in the ocean, a morning stretch in bed, dancing – lots and lots of dancing! What are the small things in your life you're grateful for?

You might think searching for more in your life, achieving more and having more will make you happier and more confident in yourself, but in reality, the key is to be grateful for who you are and what you already have. For most of us, there will always be people with more than us and people with less than us.

When you take the time to slow down and count your blessings, there are so many benefits to you and those around you. Research by Dr Robert Emmons, leading authority on gratitude and author of *Thanks! How the New Science of Gratitude Can Make You Happier*, shows that gratitude has a range of extraordinary benefits, including greater creativity, resilience, enthusiasm, determination, optimism and stronger social relationships, to name a few. Who wouldn't want more of this in their life? Ultimately, the result of all of these benefits is greater self-belief and unshakeable confidence.

As a leader, it can be challenging to find the time for self-reflection and to practise gratitude, but if you make the time for gratefulness, your relationship with yourself and others will flourish. You will be a more positive leader who is less critical of others. You will stop to celebrate the successes with your team and see the failures as opportunities to learn. Grateful for the good and the bad. You will be less stressed and less reactive in your role.

You might be sceptical about this gratitude stuff and whether it can make a real difference to how you feel about yourself, but give it a go. Gratitude is a skill and a habit you can cultivate to naturally build your self-belief and confidence.

The way you practise gratitude and make it a habit is a personal choice, but on the following page are some simple ideas.

TIPS FOR PRACTISING GRATITUDE

- **Gratitude journal:** Keep a book by your bed to jot down the things you are most grateful for. I've had journals in the past but now I have a gratitude jar (a Christmas present from my daughter, Sophie). I pop little notes in there every day. At the end of the year, I'm going to grab a glass or two of champagne and read them aloud.

- **Smile:** It's easy, costs nothing and makes you and others around you feel so good.

- **Gratitude sharing:** Ask the question, "What are you thankful for today?", at the dinner table with your family or at the start or end of a meeting with your team.

- **Thank you:** Saying these two little words more often has a big impact on you and those around you. Consider giving a handwritten note or card to someone who has made a difference in your day (maybe even a text or Snap if I'm losing you with the note/card idea!).

When you think of all of the people and experiences and factors that have unknowingly conspired to get you to exactly where you are right now, it's pretty awe-inspiring. It causes you to look at the world and the people around you in an entirely new way and to have a heightened sense of appreciation for this amazing universe in which we live.

DR PATRICIA THOMPSON

CHAPTER 5.5

Keep life light

Let it go

For a long time, I held onto things for dear life. Think white knuckles from my firm grip! I held tightly onto my marriage, my relationships with friends, my family and my job. I thought if I could hold all this down – if possible, nail it to the floor – then I would feel secure and confident. I wanted to feel in control and I thought this was the best way to go about it.

If I didn't maintain this tight grip, I felt that everything in my life would get away from me. I had a fear of losing the people and things that meant the most to me. The problem with this fear is, when things inevitably do change, it's hard to deal with and it's not pretty.

My mentor gave me some advice recently about keeping things

light in relation to building my practice and making sales, and guess what? It feels good. This concept of lightness can be applied to all aspects of our lives.

As we have explored, your grounding and confidence come from knowing yourself and believing in who you are and why you do what you do. Bear in mind that everything and everyone else is a bonus. Keeping things light changes your perspective and ensures your confidence stays strong. You think, "That new contract I received from a client? Fantastic! That cute guy I'm dating? Cool. That opportunity to speak at a conference? I love it! And I'm grateful for it – but it's not necessary. I can enjoy it, it can be rewarding, fun and fulfilling, but none of that stuff defines who I am."

When you keep things light, you know that without these extras, you are still you and you are enough. You're going to be able to carry on and move forward being you and being confident. It means you're not dependant on anyone or anything for your contentment and happiness.

Being light doesn't mean you don't care. It means accepting what you can and can't control and enjoying what is. Sometimes you just need to *let it go*. (My apologies to mums of daughters who immediately want to crawl into the foetal position when they hear that catchphrase, but it's a good one!) Let things be light and free. Yes, let things and people into your life. Welcome them in but know that they may not be there forever.

It's letting go because things happen for a reason and we need to trust this. Have you ever had the experience of something happening in your life, and at the time you're not sure why it happened but later it becomes apparent? Keeping light means accepting that some things are out of your control.

The Circles of Life[1] explain how some situations are within your control or influence, while some things simply are not. Let's look at the three circles:

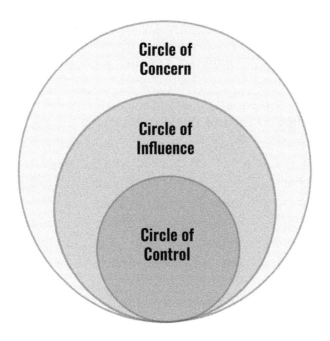

- Your **Circle of Concern** includes everything that matters to you – everything you're aware of and everything that impacts your life. Some of them you can influence and control, but others you can do nothing about. For example, the weather is something that has an impact on your life but you can't do anything to influence or control it. It's simply a concern. Yes, you can complain, whinge and criticise the things that concern you, but it won't make any difference. Best to focus your time and energy elsewhere!

1 Chittenden, C. "The Circles of Control, Influence and Concern." *Talking About*. http://www.talkingabout.com.au/3ControlInfluenceConcern

- Your **Circle of Influence** includes everything you can impact and do something about. This circle is linked to your relationships with others and the influence your actions can have on their behaviour. An example of something in your circle of influence is whether you get that next job promotion. There are things you can do that will influence this decision but in the end it's not in your control. Someone else will make that decision.

- Your **Circle of Control** includes everything you can directly make happen. These things are not dependant on anyone else, only yourself. It can be described this way: Control = Awareness + Choice. Once you are consciously aware of something, you have the power to make a choice and control the outcome. An example of something that is always in your control is your attitude. No matter what is thrown at you in life, you choose the way you respond and your attitude.

In which circle do you spend most of your time and energy?

When you feel heavy and burdened by a situation, it is worthwhile to ask yourself what about the situation sits within your circle of concern, influence and control. You have the choice about where you spend your time and energy.

It's a bit like constantly wearing a backpack. If you had to have a backpack on 24 hours a day, would you prefer it to be heavy or light? Often when I go into a meeting with a CEO, on a date with someone new or when I'm about to make a presentation, I think, "Light backpack, Midja. Keep it light and keep it playful and just be you." Whether it works out or not, whether I fail or whether I succeed, I'm still me. I'm still confident and I still believe in myself.

FOUR TIPS TO KEEP THINGS LIGHT

1. Invest in getting to know who you are. This book is the perfect start!

2. Evaluate your current relationships and commitments and ask yourself, "How do these things feel? Are they heavy or light?"

3. Consciously decide to spend less time and energy on the things that feel heavy. Loosen your grip. Take things out of that backpack and make it light.

4. Live a rich and diverse life with plenty of play involved. Engage with others, meet new people, make time for your personal interests and the stuff you love to do.

Grant me the serenity to accept
the things I cannot change;
courage to change the things
I can; and wisdom to know
the difference.

THE SERENITY PRAYER

CHAPTER 5.6

Stop the judgement

Show empathy

Have you ever had a conversation with someone and before they speak, they ask you, "OK, no judgement, right?"

I was at a lunch recently with girlfriends and a few of us asked the exact same thing. We ended up making a pact that anything could be shared at the table and it would go no further. There would be no judgement. A lot was shared at that table, let me tell you!

Sometimes my friends and I will call upon the "cone of silence" and I will even make the hand gesture that signifies we are surrounded by a glass cone. The cone of silence refers to a device from US comedy television series *Get Smart* (am I showing my age again?). It was a gadget designed for secret conversations, which, of course, never worked.

Now, when my friends and I are in the cone of silence, it means what we say is not to be repeated. More than that, it means there will be no judgement. People are only to listen, giving no opinions unless asked for them. It's a handy imaginary device! But why is it necessary?

Listening and observing without judgement can be tough. This is because we all have our unique view of the world and our own set of values. We all choose how we prioritise things in our life. Our unique view of the world is wonderful and it brings us diversity and creativity, but it can also bring judgement if we believe our view and our values are right or better than someone else's. In the words of author Stephen Covey, "We think we see the world as it is when in fact we see the world as we are."

It's like we all wear our own pair of prescription glasses. We view the world through our unique lens – ourselves, events and the people around us and what they say and what they do. Our glasses are usually held firmly in place. Each of us has a different prescription. The same event and same set of circumstances can be viewed very differently depending on your lens.

Your beliefs and values can seem so true to you that it's hard to imagine others don't see what you see. You believe your values and beliefs are right, not just for you but for everyone. Judgement happens when you think your way is the right way. You negatively judge anyone who doesn't fit into your world through their actions, words and appearance. It's so easy to do.

Perhaps making a quick judgement call has worked for you in the past. It's a coping mechanism and it's almost instinctive. Sure, sometimes a quick judgement call is the right one, but sometimes it leads to misunderstandings and communication breakdowns.

Great leadership involves taking off your glasses. If you want to gain trust as a leader and be someone who can connect with others, you must understand other people's points of view. Empathy is a must-have leadership trait. If you let the judgement go, you will feel more at ease with others and you'll gain a greater understanding of them. Of course, you may not always agree with them and you may not ever fully understand them, but you won't stand in judgement of them.

When I was leading a legal team, there was a particular law clerk who was outstanding at her job and who I thought had huge potential. I discussed excitedly with her the process of starting her studies in law and becoming admitted as a solicitor. It was the path to partnership and I thought she would share my enthusiasm about climbing the corporate ladder. When she told me she had no intention of ever studying law and was very happy in her role as a clerk, I looked at her in bewilderment. I asked her, "What do you mean you don't want to become a partner of a law firm? Isn't that why you're working here?" And her response was a simple no.

It took me some time to realise my own beliefs, legacy and ambitions were just that – *my own*! Not everyone wants what you want. As a leader, it is so tempting to project your thoughts onto others. It can come from a very good intention, but the impact is that the other person feels judged and inadequate, like they're not living up to your expectations.

Let's face it, people know when they're being judged. You can sense it. It makes them close up and stop sharing. They stop being authentic because they feel your judgement and disapproval.

If you deeply know yourself and believe in yourself, judging others isn't necessary. You don't need to build yourself up by putting others down and judging them by your standards. As a leader, you can be inquisitive and curious, knowing that what others say and do is because of who they are – and they are, of course, different to you. No better or worse, just different. And difference is good.

Often when you judge others, it's not about the person you're judging at all. It's about you. It comes from a lack of self-belief. Something the other person has said or done makes you feel uncomfortable or makes you defensive. It doesn't match your expectations. It's like holding a mirror up to yourself and revealing a part of yourself you may not want to see, causing feelings you might not want to feel. If you find yourself starting to judge someone else, stop and get some space to think about what has triggered that response.

Of course, others may judge you, your behaviour and your appearance, and I say let them. Other people's opinions aren't in your circle of control. The only person you can control is yourself.

Now, we've spoken a lot about judging others, but perhaps the worst judgement of all is the judgement we make about ourselves. Give yourself a break and stop being so self-critical. Often, the things you say to yourself you wouldn't dare say to anyone else. So, don't be so harsh. You're doing your best with what you know and what you have at this time.

You can and will make mistakes. You'll do things you will shake your head over. You will get out that baseball bat in your back pocket, and we all have one there. Some of us have a different size bat, depending on the level we beat ourselves up. You might find yourself thinking you should have done something differently, but the great thing is you can learn from your mistakes. Self-reflection is great if you do it from a neutral place, observing yourself and what happened without being too harsh.

The best gift you can give to yourself and to others is to take off your prescription glasses and let go of judgement. See the best in everyone, including yourself, and practise genuine empathy.

QUESTIONS FOR YOU TO CONSIDER IN YOUR LEADERSHIP ROLE

1. Are you curious and inquisitive as a leader?

   _____

   _____

   _____

2. Do you see the potential and unique contribution in each of your team members?

   _____

   _____

   _____

3. How do you ensure your people feel valued and appreciated?

   _____

   _____

   _____

   _____

4. Can you become possessive of your beliefs and ideas?

   _____

   _____

   _____

   _____

5. How do you ensure that everyone in your team has an equal voice?

_____

_____

_____

_____

6. Do you jump in and solve problems or do you take the time to understand the real issue?

_____

_____

_____

_____

7. Do you spend more time being the expert or being the coach?

_____

_____

_____

_____

8. Are you open to receiving honest feedback from others?

_____

_____

_____

_____

9. Do you give honest and helpful feedback to others?

_____

_____

_____

_____

10. Are you loyal to the absent or do you talk about people behind their back?

_____

_____

_____

_____

If you judge people, you have no time to love them.

MOTHER TERESA

CHAPTER 5.7

Take action and repeat

Repetition will change your thinking

I've been single for a little while now. Welcome to dating in your 40s! (I'm sure there's another book on that whole topic!)

When I first started dating after having been with my husband for close to 20 years, it was daunting. Before a date, all sorts of questions would run through my head: what will he think about how I look, are we going to have anything to talk about, will there be awkward silences, is he going to take one look at me and leave? I was making assumptions and I was down the bottom of the confidence tree. I didn't know who I was as a single woman and I was completely lost.

What to do about these feelings? What to do about my lack of self-belief in the dating world? What I did was I kept going on dates.

CHAPTER 5.7

I figured I wasn't going to meet anyone sitting at home on my couch, so I got out there and dated – coffee dates, dinner dates, getting out there and meeting new people. And you know what? It got easier. A lot easier.

Now when I go on a date, that fear and negative self-talk are no longer there. I remember going on a date at one of my favourite restaurants, Pier on the Spit. I parked the car and waited until I got the green light – the text that says, "I'm outside the restaurant." So, with one last check in the mirror and a deep breath, I said, "Let's do this."

I got out of my car and as I walked towards the restaurant, my shoulders were back, my head held high and I was smiling. I love that anticipation as you walk towards someone. They look at you and you look at them, waiting to see if there is any magic. Maybe I'm just a hopeless romantic.

I haven't found that magic yet but I have found my confidence when it comes to dating and it's an altogether different experience.

Stepping into a leadership position feels the same way. At the beginning, you're worried about what others think of you and you're unsure whether you can fulfil the role (the imposter syndrome we spoke about in Chapter 1). It's the first time you've presented at a senior leadership meeting, it's the first time you've chaired your own team meeting or run a coaching session. Everything is unfamiliar and you feel out of your depth. Amy Cuddy, social psychologist and Harvard Business School professor (check out Cuddy's TED Talk, "Your body language shapes who you are"), says that when it comes to building confidence, "It's not fake it until you make it. It's fake it until you become it."

You can justify your inaction to yourself and others with a whole bunch of excuses. Excuses like, "I'm waiting for help", "I don't know where to begin", "It won't work", and the common one I hear and have said myself many times as a leader, "I don't have the right resources." If you find yourself using these excuses, it's time to focus on what you can do instead of what you can't and be open to possibilities. It's time to move forward.

Growing your self-belief and gaining confidence take action. You can't sit still. You need to do *something* to change your self-belief and you must keep doing it. Repetition is the key.

To change your beliefs about an event, set of circumstances or even yourself, you must take action because if nothing changes, then nothing changes. The lawyer in me likens it to a court case – you need to prove to yourself, to that self-doubter in your head, that she's wrong. Your self-talk, your inner judge, needs evidence. She's screaming at you, *"Show me the evidence before I change your mind. You want to believe this dating is fun, that it's an opportunity to meet new people? Then, get out there and show me and once you show me, I'll change my view on it and change your thoughts."*

It's a chicken-and-egg argument. Which comes first – your actions or your beliefs? I think you can attack self-confidence from both angles. Sometimes it will be your way of thinking that changes your behaviour but other times, repeating an action and getting a different result will change your thinking about it.

Do you remember going on a rollercoaster for the first time? What happened? Let's go back.

You're sweating in the queue, thinking this is not a great idea. You try to see if you can discreetly slip out of the line, but before you realise it, you're at the front of the queue and it's time to get in. You step into the ride and you're strapped in tight. You're breathing heavily and the adrenaline runs through you, and you hold on for dear life. The rollercoaster starts, your knuckles are white. Your eyes are shut tight for the entire time and you're screaming, or perhaps you're so afraid you can't even scream. But guess what happens? The ride finishes and you didn't die. Ha! Interesting.

Let's go on the rollercoaster again. This time, your grip is a bit looser. You open your eyes occasionally. And when the ride finishes, you think to yourself, "I actually enjoyed that. Let's go on it again."

The third time you go on the rollercoaster, your hands fly up in excitement. You squeal with delight, your eyes are open and you're loving it!

It's the same with any fear or self-doubt in your life. It takes action to change it, even if that action is a baby step. At first, it will probably feel awkward and uncomfortable. As I've said before, you need to get comfortable with being uncomfortable. You might feel like giving up, particularly if you don't see immediate results, but repetition will make the difference. It will get better and you will find out what you are capable of.

It's those mixed feelings of fear and excitement that make you feel alive. It's the spot where you know you're on the cusp of doing something awesome. You get to shake things up and you get to significantly grow your self-belief and confidence.

DO YOU NEED TO TAKE ACTION?

1. Think about something in your life right now that you would like to accomplish but feels out of reach.

    _____

    _____

    _____

2. Why does it feel out of reach? Are these excuses getting in the way of your goal?

    _____

    _____

    _____

3. What's the impact of doing nothing?

    _____

    _____

    _____

4. What's the value of taking action? What does accomplishing the goal look like? How does it feel?

    _____

    _____

    _____

5. List all the things you could do to step closer towards that accomplishment.

_____

_____

_____

_____

_____

6. From the list, what's one action you can take *today*?

_____

_____

_____

_____

7. Do that! (and the next day and the next day and the next day ...)

_____

_____

_____

_____

Every day do something that will inch you closer to a better tomorrow.

DOUG FIREBAUGH

CHAPTER 5.8

Let go of others' expectations

Push the "shoulds" to one side

When I practised law, people always reacted similarly when I told them what I did for work. No matter if it was at a barbecue, dinner or networking event, this is how the conversation would usually go:

Them: So, what do you do for work?

Me: Well, I'm a lawyer, a partner of a national law firm.

Them: Good one. So, what do you really do? (Chuckling)

Me: Seriously, I'm a lawyer.

Them: Wow, you don't look or act like one.

CHAPTER 5.8

This is the conversation I would have over and over with people, and it would always leave me thinking; as a lawyer, how do they expect me to look and behave? And how come I'm not living up to those expectations? Do they mean it in a good way or a bad way? I wasn't sure.

You see, people will have expectations of you. Expectations of you as a leader, as a woman, as a woman of your age, as a wife and as a mother. If you take all those expectations on board, if you try to live up to them, you will start to feel their weight upon you.

Expectations can cage you in. You feel like you can't move, you can't breathe. You feel heavy and trapped. You feel like you can't be yourself.

But when you stop focussing on others and turn your focus inward, when you know yourself and can be true to yourself, you free yourself of the cage. You might feel shaky at first, a little uncertain and overwhelmed because you need to reconnect with yourself. "Who am I and what do I want?" But when you work that out, like a caged tiger that is finally set free, you'll be able to run and it will feel exhilarating.

It can be tough to let go of the expectations of others, particularly of those people who are closest to you, but you need to stop trying to be everything to everyone. Don't stop being yourself just because other people expect something different.

You might want to change because you want to please others. You don't want to disappoint anyone. You want to say yes because you want to be liked. You want to be validated and accepted. But listening to other people's expectations and changing yourself because of them means you can start to lose your sense of identity. You second guess yourself, self-doubt starts creeping in and your confidence flounders.

Women often use the phrase, "I should ...": I should go to the gym more often, I should do part-time study, I should spend more time with my kids. Whenever I hear someone use that phrase, I always ask the question, "*Who* thinks you should?" And the answer is "*they*" do.

So, who are "they"? Sometimes "they" can be your parents, your partner or your colleagues, but sometimes "they" refers to a society norm you have bought into. Don't let "them" take control of your life and dictate what you do and don't do with your time. Don't feel guilty for not following their rules. Don't let them change you into someone you're not. Don't let them impact your self-belief and confidence. You'll only be putting on a show and not living with authenticity. It will be exhausting and, at some point, you will start to feel resentful, as though you are living the life of someone else.

Only one person's expectations matter: yours. The expectations you have placed on yourself by knowing yourself and by understanding your story, values and purpose are the only ones you should listen to. By keeping these front of mind, you can leave your legacy and make the difference you are meant to make.

So, push the "shoulds" to one side and ask yourself, "What do I want? What will make me happy and fulfilled?"

Remember who you were before the world told you who you should be!

TIPS FOR LETTING GO OF OTHERS' EXPECTATIONS

- Be willing to make mistakes and learn from them.

- Speak up and own your voice.

- Listen to your intuition.

- Remember that no one knows you better than you know yourself.

- Do things your way, according to your values.

- Be willing to go it alone without handholding.

- Spend time with people who value you.

- Don't let others' opinions define your reality.

- Embrace your uniqueness – what makes you *you*.

- Less "I should" and more "I want".

I'm going to pay attention to the reality of my life and the audacity of my dreams instead of the expectation I was raised with.

TRACEE ELLIS ROSS

CHAPTER 5.9

Change your self-talk

Create useful beliefs about you

The most important words you will ever say are the words you say to yourself. It's that little voice in your head, your inner dialogue, that significantly impacts your level of self-belief.

So, what stories do you tell yourself? What's the script running through your head? How do you truly feel when you look in the mirror? What limits have you put in place?

You can talk yourself into or out of anything. When you put negative thoughts into your conscious mind, you start to act a certain way. What you think impacts your behaviour, and it's easy to only see the negative side of yourself.

It's critical we challenge our negative thoughts. A study conducted by Michigan State University found that the average person has 80,000 thoughts per day, 80% of which are negative.[1] What's going on? We need to change our thinking so we can change the results we get in our lives. Positive thinking will result in positive action.

The great news is, we can regain control of our thinking. We have a brilliant goal-seeking part of our brains called the reticular activating system, or RAS for short. We can program our RAS to help us achieve our goals. This part of the brain wants us to be right, so it brings to our attention the things that are important to us and discards everything else. Because we are faced with so much information and noise every day, and we couldn't possibly take it all in, our RAS acts like a filter. We program it and it filters what we see, then helps guide what we do. So, when you think something and believe it, you make it come true. You look everywhere for evidence of it and you find it. It's a self-fulfilling prophecy.

Have you ever been guilty of focussing only on the negative? A million things could have happened in your day, but you focus on the one thing that didn't go so well. That's the way you've programmed your RAS.

Let's say you think you're not the best person for a new leadership position. If this is the way you think, you behave correspondingly. You may not speak up at the next managers meeting. You may not put the time into the application process. You might even share your negative thoughts with other colleagues, then you'll start reading into others' behaviours to confirm your thoughts. Suddenly, the email that was missed by your general manager means she doesn't value your work, which means you're not important enough, which means she doesn't want you to get the

---

1 Millett, M. "Challenge your negative thoughts." *Extension*, Michigan State University, 31 March, 2017. http://msue.anr.msu.edu/news/challenge_your_negative_thoughts

leadership position. And guess what happens next? You don't get the position. You were right. You thought it, you put energy into it, your focus was purely on the negative, then bingo – that's what you got. The negative. Congratulations.

To break it down:

Thought -> energy -> manifestation

Your thoughts are more powerful than you think. Thankfully, your thoughts are in your circle of control. You get to choose your thinking and, importantly, how you think about yourself.

On my 43rd birthday, I started the day with a yoga class with my friend, Toni, the instructor. We started as usual with our warm-up, breathing exercises, downward dog and warrior pose, then it got to that part of the class I really didn't like – the headstand practice. I had never done a headstand before. I had seen other yogis in the class balance on their heads and I'd look at them and want to do it, but it just didn't seem physically possible for me. That's what I told myself.

However, during this class on my birthday, something changed. I decided to give it a shot. Toni was by my side encouraging me, talking me through it, getting me to tighten my core, helping me get my balance, and guess what? I did it.

There I was, on the mat doing a headstand. OK, it may have been for three seconds, but I've got a photo to prove it. You know the thing that changed? It was my self-talk. There was something about it being my birthday and everything else going on in my life that made me think, "Midja, you can do this. You've got this."

You may be thinking, a headstand, big deal. I get that. But for me, getting into that headstand position became super important – symbolic almost. It wasn't the physical act that mattered, it was what it stood for. For months, I had firmly believed it was something I would never be able to do, but I did it. I walked away from that class thinking, "If I didn't think I could do a headstand and I did, what else can I do? What limits have I placed on myself that I don't even realise?"

I remember my Mum reminding me that if you can't say something nice, don't say anything at all. I think this applies firstly to what you say about yourself. If you have negative thoughts about yourself, if you talk to yourself in a damaging way, then you'll never gain the self-belief you need to achieve your goals as a leader. You'll only be limiting yourself. If you catch yourself slipping into those negative thoughts – "I'm not good enough, I'll never get that promotion" – swap them for kind, beautiful words. Be gentle with yourself.

By getting to know yourself intimately, you will get to know your strengths and magic so you can focus your thoughts and energy on them. You can transform your negative and limiting beliefs into useful, motivating beliefs – beliefs that are authentic and tap into the real you. Every time you recite those positive beliefs, you reaffirm and strengthen them. They will bring about positive action because you make it so much easier for your RAS to see evidence all around you that supports your self-belief.

Before you can become a confident leader, you must think like one. You need to create that image of yourself, the leader you aspire to be.

QUESTIONS TO ASK YOURSELF ABOUT THE LEADER YOU WANT TO BE

1. What does she look like?

_____

_____

_____

_____

2. How does she feel?

_____

_____

_____

_____

3. What does she say and do?

_____

_____

_____

_____

4. How does she inspire and influence others?

_____

_____

_____

_____

*Talk to yourself like you would
to someone you love.*

BRENÉ BROWN

CHAPTER 5.10

Take the compliment

Thank you very much

It was a Saturday afternoon and Mum and I had decided to take my daughter, Sophie, who was four or five years old at the time, on a shopping trip. We went to Marina Mirage on the Gold Coast. We were browsing a clothes shop when the assistant came up to Sophie and said, "Well, you're a gorgeous little girl. You have the most beautiful hair I've ever seen." Sophie smiled, looked at the shop assistant and said, "Yes, I know. Thanks."

Oh, my goodness! As a mum, I was so embarrassed by her response. I mean, it's not what we say, is it? We don't go around saying, "Yes, I know I'm beautiful." However, along with my embarrassment, I also felt in awe of her confidence, her self-assuredness. It made me think about what I do when I receive a compliment, and I started to observe what my friends say and do when I give them one.

CHAPTER 5.10

Do you know what happens when women receive a compliment? We reject it, usually in one of three ways. Say someone says, "You look gorgeous in that dress, I love it!" Response number one is a self-put down: "What? This old thing? It's years old. Actually, it's been getting a bit tight. I must have put on some weight." Response number two is a deflection: "My dress? No, I was just thinking how gorgeous *your* dress looks." And response number three highlights our inner sceptic: "Really? You think? I'm not so sure."

Do any of these responses sound familiar? I know I've heard myself and many of my friends and colleagues say them. When someone gives you a compliment, these responses become automatic. You've created a habit and you don't even know you're saying it.

Why do you sometimes find it hard to accept a compliment? Why do you bat it away and put your walls up? Firstly, it might be because you don't want to appear arrogant or cocky. In Australian culture, we call it the tall poppy syndrome. Even if we are confident and we want to believe the compliment, we refuse to accept it because we don't want to appear conceited.

Secondly, it might be that you simply don't have enough self-belief to be able to accept the compliment. It doesn't make sense to you. It clashes with your self-talk, your inner dialogue, your view of the world. Someone tells you you're beautiful but you think you're not. Therefore, you feel the need to bat it away. If you let the compliment in, you won't know what to do with it, it won't sit nicely with the other messages you hold onto. The trick, of course, is to change your self-talk and allow the compliment to strengthen and reaffirm your positive self-belief.

Think of compliments as extra nourishment for your confidence tree. They provide additional fertiliser, an extra bit of watering, some sunshine. You don't need compliments and the affirmations of others to be confident, but they do add to your growth. They're beautiful things.

Being gracious and accepting a compliment is a great way to boost your influence as a leader in a genuine and authentic way. Why wouldn't you grab that opportunity? As a leader, when you fail to take a compliment and respond to it in one of the three ways described, it can impact your credibility and reputation. For example, if you deflect or question a compliment on the way you presented at a meeting or your ability to stay calm in a difficult situation, your people might start to question you. "Well, maybe she isn't that great a presenter," or, "Maybe that was just a once off when she was calm in that situation." They will start to second guess you and change their perception of you. But when you accept a compliment, it reaffirms your strengths to your people. It adds to your personal brand. Think of it as a great testimonial – take it and use it.

Furthermore, if you fail to accept a compliment, you not only miss the opportunity to get that extra nourishment, you can impact the relationship you have with the person who gave you the compliment. When someone goes out of their way to give you positive feedback, they're trying to make a connection with you and build rapport. When you reject it, you reject their attempt to connect. When you think about it, it can be downright rude. Someone gives you the gift of a compliment and you give it back to them? It's not that you intend to do this, of course, but you make it known you're only thinking about yourself. You're so caught up in your thoughts, you don't even think about the impact your rejection could have on the other person.

Let's switch it around. When you give someone a compliment,

you mean it, right? It's genuine. You want the other person to open their arms, open their hearts and accept it. People want the same response from you.

It's time to get as much positivity and feel-good vibes in your life as you can. So, when someone hands you a compliment, grab it with both hands. Instead of downplaying your accomplishments, intellect and looks, celebrate what makes you exceptional. Remember, people see amazing things in you – because you *are* amazing.

WHAT YOU CAN DO WITH YOUR NEXT COMPLIMENT

- Firstly, notice it. Don't ignore it.

- Before reacting to the compliment, pause, take it in.

- Respond with a simple thank you. Maybe leave out the "I know" that my daughter added in, but acknowledge and thank the person for their compliment.

- Say something genuine and positive in response.

A strong woman accepts both compliments and criticism graciously, knowing that it takes both sunshine and rain for a flower to grow.

MANDY HALE

CHAPTER 6

UNSHAKEABLE

CHAPTER 6

Unshakeable

unshakeable
adjective used to describe YOU
1. The highest level of confidence.
"An unshakeable woman."
Synonyms: steadfast, strong, blazing, resolute, determined, unwavering, impactful.

Congratulations! You are now at the top of the confidence tree and unshakeable. You have done the hard work to truly get to know yourself intimately. You can be authentic in any situation and you have an unwavering self-belief.

THE UNSHAKEABLE LOOK

You walk into a room and people notice you. People can see and sense your confidence. You're confident not in an ego-driven "look at me" way, but people can see your self-assurance and self-belief.

You walk tall and poised with your shoulders back. You make eye contact, you smile and you have a lightness about you.

Your confidence comes from within and that makes it untouchable. It radiates from you. It announces to the world that this is who you are and you make no apologies for being you. You are real and authentic.

People see in you a beautiful balance of courage and consideration. In other words, you have the strength to be yourself and have your own opinions and viewpoints, but you are also mindful of others and show empathy and understanding.

You have a formidable tribe surrounding you – people who support you in everything you do and who share your self-belief.

Your confidence doesn't need to be gregarious and loud – not at all. It can be quiet and calm, but it is always strong and always felt by others.

THE UNSHAKEABLE FEELING

You feel comfortable in your skin. More than this, you relish being you. You feel great about yourself. I remember as a young girl, when people asked me who I would like to be, I never understood the question because I never wanted to be anyone but me. You don't, either!

You feel light and free. You don't have to pretend to be someone you're not. You're open and vulnerable and loving it. You find joy in everyday moments.

Along with this lightness you feel, you have a determined and tenacious resolution to live true to your values and make the difference you were meant to make. Your authenticity and self-belief give you the power to follow your dreams and live the life you want. You have a clear purpose and a fulfilled and meaningful life.

You are positive and optimistic. You know nothing is impossible.

THE UNSHAKEABLE IMPACT

Confidence is easy to catch. When you're unshakeable, you pass your confidence on to other people. They see you as an inspiration. As a mother, you pass it on to your kids; as a friend, to your tribe; as a leader, to your team members and your whole organisation.

When you're unshakeable, people want to be around you. There is an unexplainable, irresistible something about you, and that something is your *confidence*. It's all the work you have done on yourself. Your authenticity shines through and it makes people feel that they can be themselves, too. They can be vulnerable, take a risk and make a mistake.

THE UNSHAKEABLE LEADER

As a leader, you are collaborative rather than competitive. When you're confident in yourself, you don't have to be right about everything. You know your leadership strengths and weaknesses and can accept when you're wrong and when you need help.

You don't feel threatened by the competency of those around you. You recognise and celebrate the strengths of others. There is an attitude of abundance. In your team, there is no token reward system but authentic gratitude and thankfulness for the work and contribution of others. Your people feel this, it motivates them, it makes them want to belong to your tribe, and they want to follow you.

Confidence changes your focus as a leader. You can now give your attention to being of service to others because you no longer worry about yourself and what others think of you. You give your opinions freely without fear of judgement or rejection, and you accept criticism and feedback.

You lead with purpose and integrity and you know exactly what you bring to the leadership table. You have a clear legacy that drives your decision making. You don't pretend to be someone you're not and you no longer feel you must hide or tone down your feminine qualities. You have your own style and brand of leadership and you challenge the traditional masculine view of what it takes to be a strong leader. Your strength as a leader comes from knowing who you are, being authentic and believing that you *are* a leader.

SO, WHAT'S NEXT?

Yes, you're at the top of the confidence tree and unshakeable, but the work is not done yet. You can't tick your confidence box and expect to stay there. Confidence is a habit: it requires you to practise the rituals of knowing yourself, being yourself and believing in yourself.

Things will change. When you go out into the world to make the difference you were meant to make, you'll come across obstacles and challenges that will require you to focus on self-renewal. Your confidence tree will need to be tended and fertilised. When life throws a lot at you, you will need to prop it up.

Sometimes your confidence tree will need a good prune. You will need to cut it back to reassess your priorities in life – your relationships, work projects, career, interests and where you spend your time. But this pruning will create new growth.

Sometimes your confidence tree will be in full season, filled with flowers and fruit. Other times, it won't be and that's OK. There's a season for everything. It's important you continue to get to know yourself, your values and your beliefs. Keep working on the legacy you want to leave, the difference you want to make in the world, and above all keep believing in yourself.

So, get out there and be unshakeable.

Be magnificent and show the world what you can do.

Celebrate the amazing woman you are.

Hold your head high, your shoulders back, and smile.

Be your confident and brilliant self.

It's time to take your seat at the leadership table!

I am not afraid.
I was born to do this.

JOAN OF ARC

AN INVITATION

An invitation

Now that you have read the book, I'd like to extend an invitation to you to join my **Women with CONFIDENCE Leadership Program**.

This national program is designed for talented professional women who want to become courageous, unshakeable leaders. It will empower you to take action on everything you've learnt within these pages.

When working with women, I commonly find that negative self-talk, critical self-judgement, self-doubt and the constant pursuit of perfection and balance hold them back from gaining the confidence they need to succeed. When you combine these factors with the unintentional gender biases often found in the workplace, it is not hard to see why women suffer from "the imposter syndrome".

The solution? A mentoring program for women that builds their confidence and inspires them to be great leaders.

This program will connect you with a tribe of likeminded women and create a space of high trust to share your story, your problems and your fears, and also your triumphs. It will give you the time and space you need to get to know yourself again, get clear about your next move and develop the attitude and skills to take your seat at the leadership table.

As a result of the program, you will:

- Double your confidence as a leader.
- Gain a deep level of self-awareness and purpose.
- Create an authentic leadership brand to increase your presence.
- Develop a powerful leadership mindset and skillset to step up in your career.

I can't wait to meet you, support you and help you to become unshakeable.

Find out more at
www.midja.com.au

Midja x

You are strong but together we are stronger.

 FISHER

Midja is an authentic, engaging and powerful speaker and facilitator. Her leadership program, "Women with Confidence", is perfect for professional women who want to grow their confidence to become courageous and unshakeable leaders.

Midja delivers corporate programs in leadership and company culture with high impact and energy. Her programs create lasting change and sustainable outcomes for her clients.

- Book Midja to speak at your next conference.
- Join the Women with Confidence leadership program.
- Check out Midja's corporate programs.
- Subscribe to Midja's weekly video blog, "Mondays with Midja".
- Follow, like and connect.

Become unshakeable!

 LINKEDIN
www.linkedin.com/in/midja/

 FACEBOOK
www.facebook.com/midja.leadership

 INSTAGRAM
www.instagram.com/midja_fisher/

www.midja.com.au
midja@midja.com.au
0408 718 445

Lightning Source UK Ltd.
Milton Keynes UK
UKHW011207140421
381978UK00001B/295